Melissa Forney's
PICTURE SPELLER
FOR YOUNG WRITERS

Written by Melissa Forney
Illustrated by John Bianchi

To my mother, who taught me that "library" has an "r" in it!
MWF

To Margie, who always gets the spelling right.
JAB

When I was a girl, I loved to write. I wrote about everything! I spied on the neighbors and kept notebooks on what they did. I wrote songs about wanting to own a horse with a flowing mane and tail. I wrote original plays and directed huge productions with my friends as the stars. I even wrote a message in a bottle, set it adrift in the Pacific Ocean, and hoped it would be found by a girl my age in China.

Kids love to write! Kids can write beautiful stories, reports, plays, poems, photo captions, e-mails, and essays. Expressing oneself in writing is a skill, so young authors need practice to develop their skill. The problem is, some kids need help with spelling. Anyone who has taught writing has heard the familiar phrase, "How do you spell this word?"

This book has been designed to help children become independent writers. By looking at the pictures, they can figure out how to spell the words on their own. The words are arranged by themes. This gives kids a "chunk" of words to choose from, all on a given topic. The variety of words reminds children of other words they can use to express thoughts and enhance their writing. What a resource!

Compiling the list of words and working with the illustrator has been a lot of fun. In my opinion, John Bianchi is a genius! He took my ideas and made them come alive through his creative drawings and vivid colors. We both enjoyed putting the book together. Now we hope even the youngest writers will find it a valuable tool to help them become fantastic, expressive writers and authors.

Melissa Forney

Table of Contents

Table of Contents

Author's Note to Teachers and Parents

This book has been designed to be used by children, young writers, primary and intermediate readers, and those learning English from another language background. We have grouped over 1300 pictures into themes. The themes are in random order, all subjects that should be of interest to kids. Within the themes we have placed the words and terms in alphabetical order except for a few pages that made more sense to group in logical order. Great care has been given in choosing these particular words and to research correct spellings, terms, and usage.

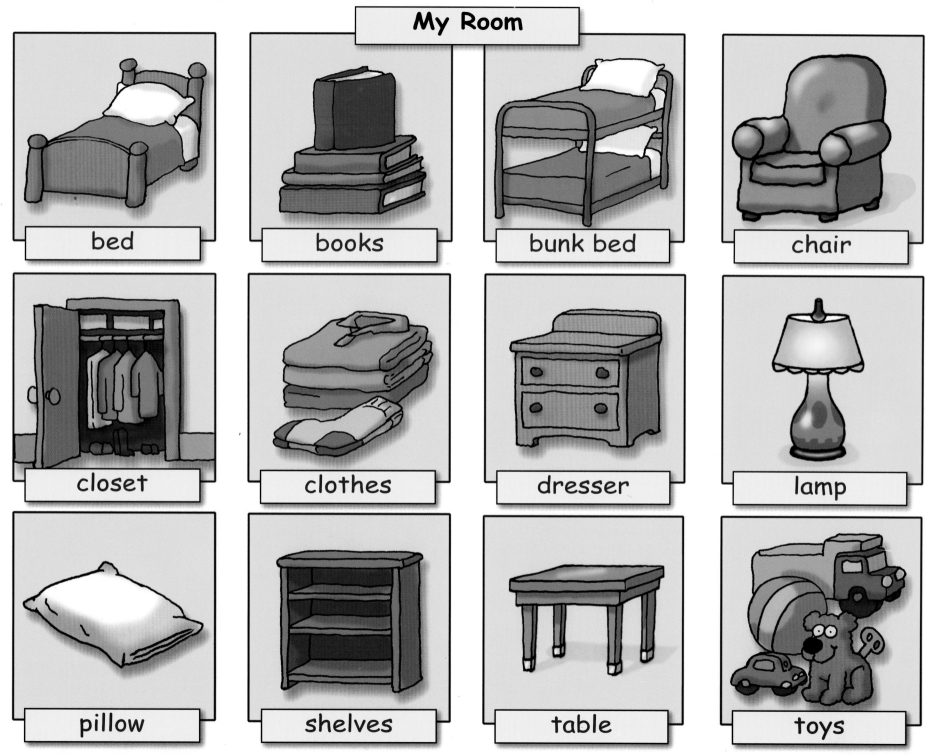

My Room

bed

books

bunk bed

chair

closet

clothes

dresser

lamp

pillow

shelves

table

toys

1

The Beach

bathing suit

beach

boat

boogie board

bucket

crab

fish

float

ocean

palm tree

sailboat

sand

The Beach

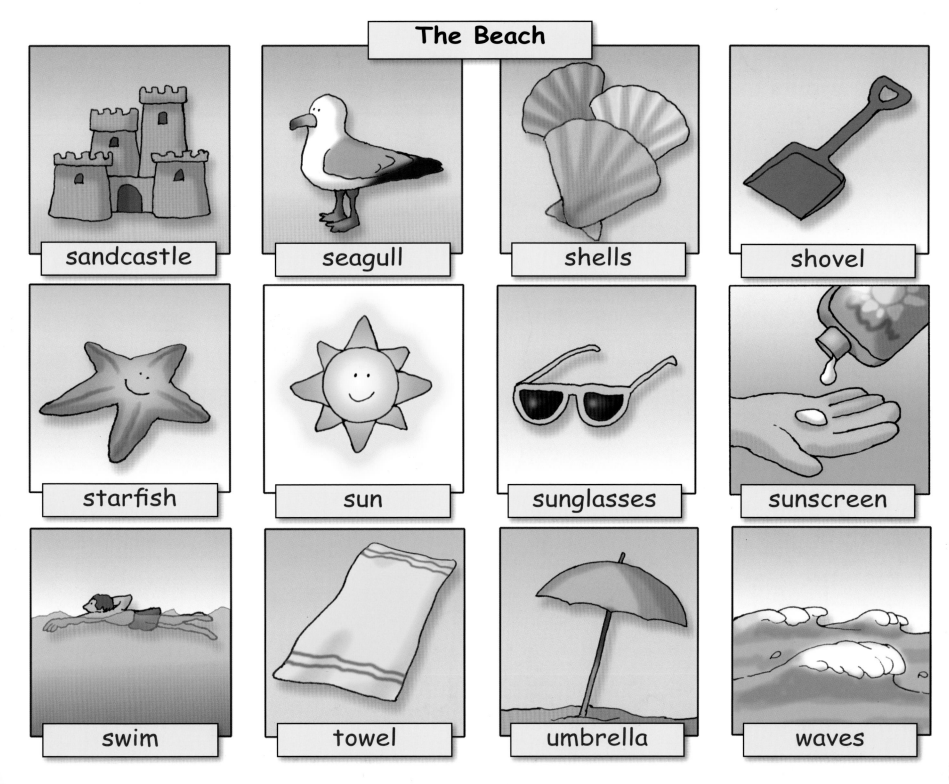

sandcastle

seagull

shells

shovel

starfish

sun

sunglasses

sunscreen

swim

towel

umbrella

waves

3

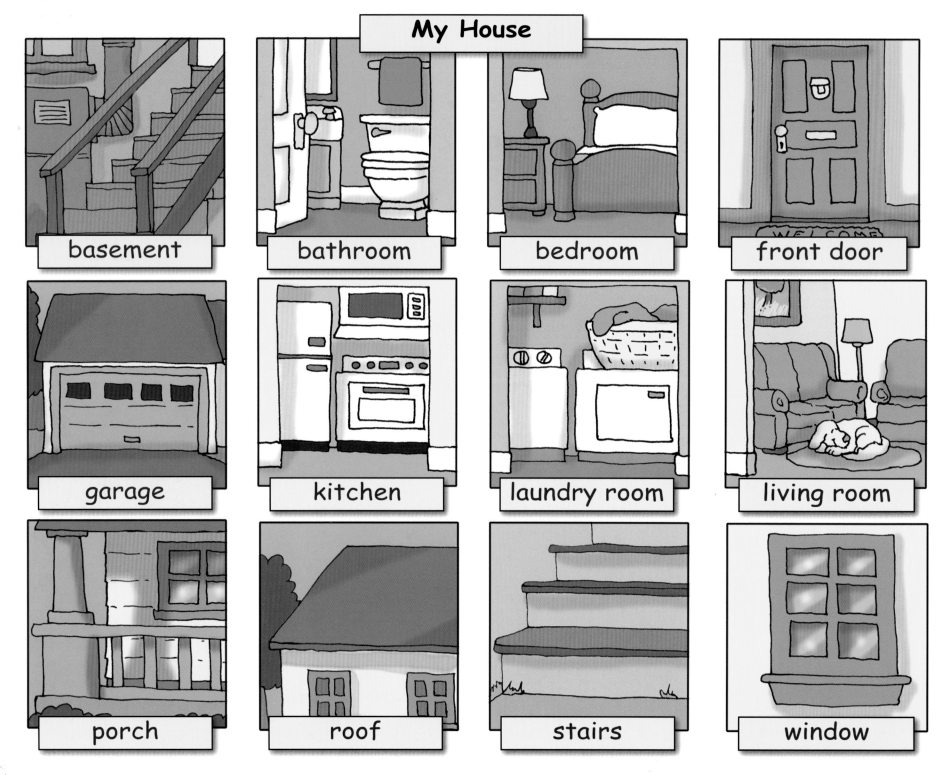

My House

basement

bathroom

bedroom

front door

garage

kitchen

laundry room

living room

porch

roof

stairs

window

4

Our School

art room

bus

cafeteria

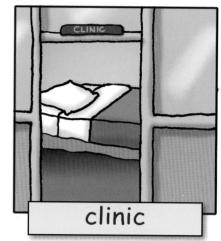
clinic

gym

hall

library

music room

office

playground

principal

secretary

5

Our Class

aquarium	backpack	board	books
chair	computer	crayons	desk
eraser	flag	globe	lunchbox

6

Our Class

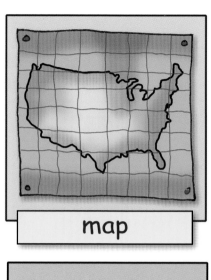

map

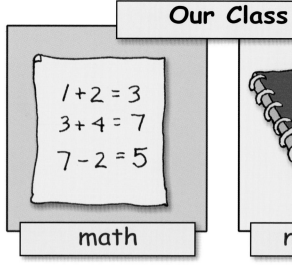

math

notebook

paper

pencil

reading

science

scissors

sharpener

student

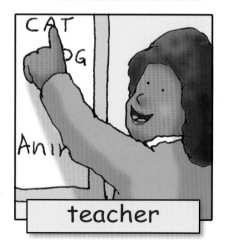

teacher

writing

The Playground

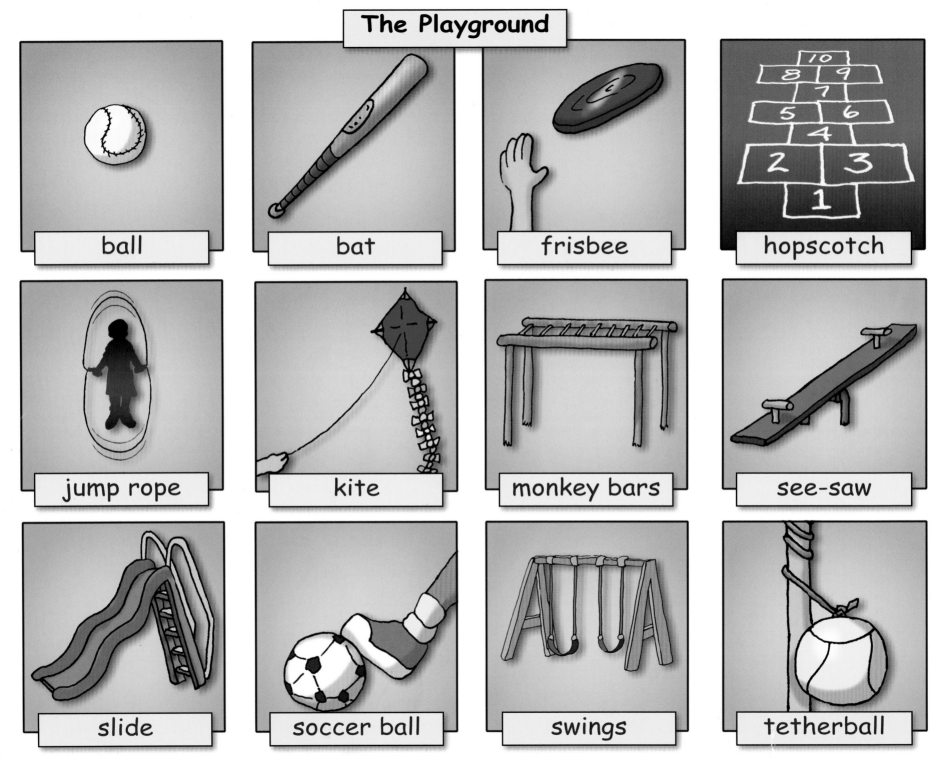

ball

bat

frisbee

hopscotch

jump rope

kite

monkey bars

see-saw

slide

soccer ball

swings

tetherball

8

The Farm

barn

chicken

cow

dog

farmer

field

goat

hay

horse

pig

rooster

tractor

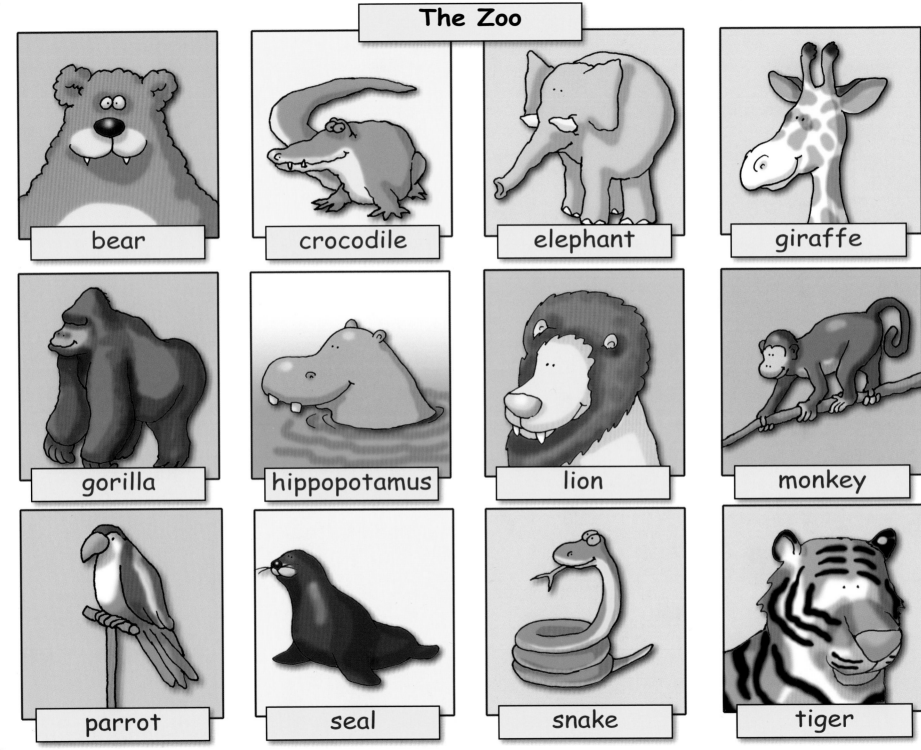

The Zoo

bear

crocodile

elephant

giraffe

gorilla

hippopotamus

lion

monkey

parrot

seal

snake

tiger

10

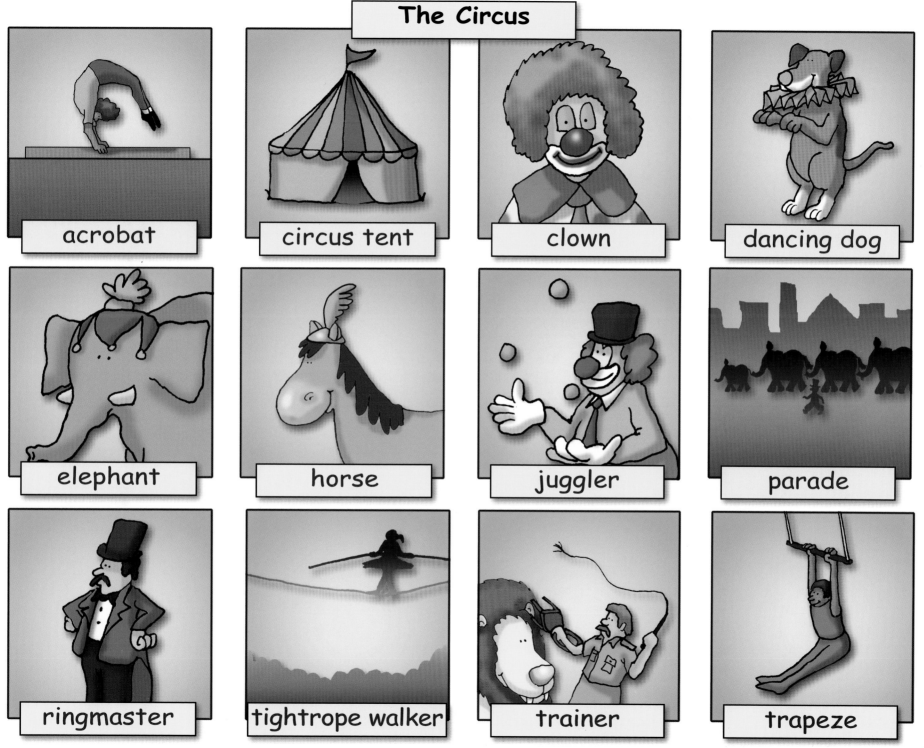

The Circus

acrobat

circus tent

clown

dancing dog

elephant

horse

juggler

parade

ringmaster

tightrope walker

trainer

trapeze

11

Space

astronaut

blast off

comet

Earth

galaxy

Martian

moon

planets

rocket

space station

stars

sun

The Rainforest

butterfly

canopy

ferns

flower

jungle

monkey

parrot

pool

toucan

tree

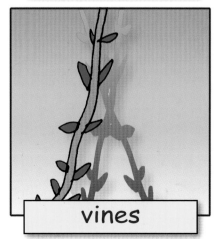
vines

waterfall

13

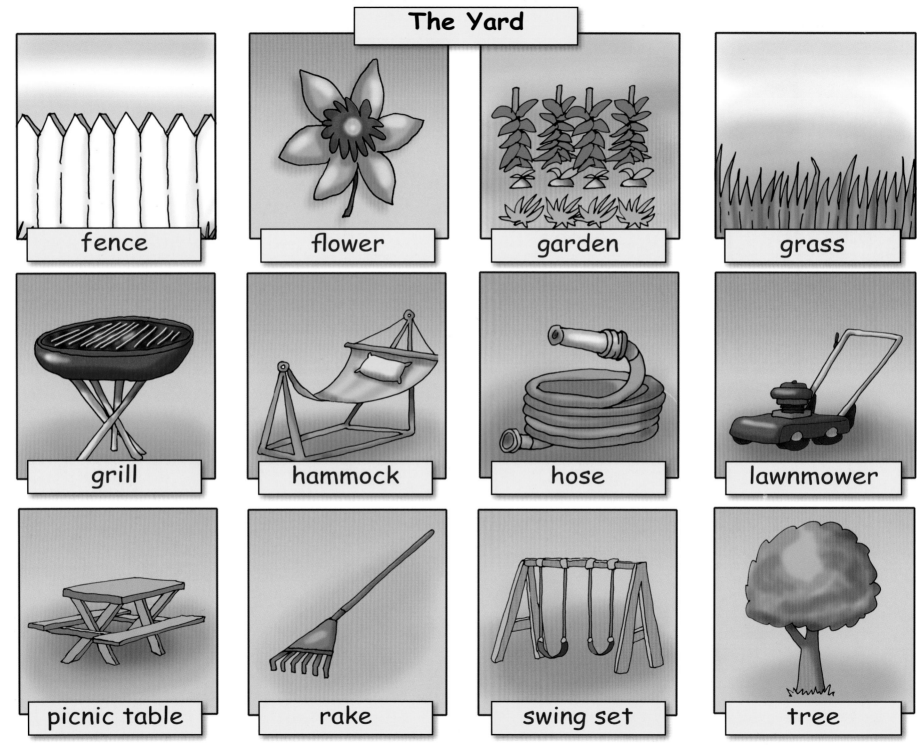

The Yard

fence

flower

garden

grass

grill

hammock

hose

lawnmower

picnic table

rake

swing set

tree

14

The Gym

balance beam

basketball

bleachers

cheerleader

coach

goal

gymnastics

mat

pom-poms

scoreboard

somersault

tumbling

15

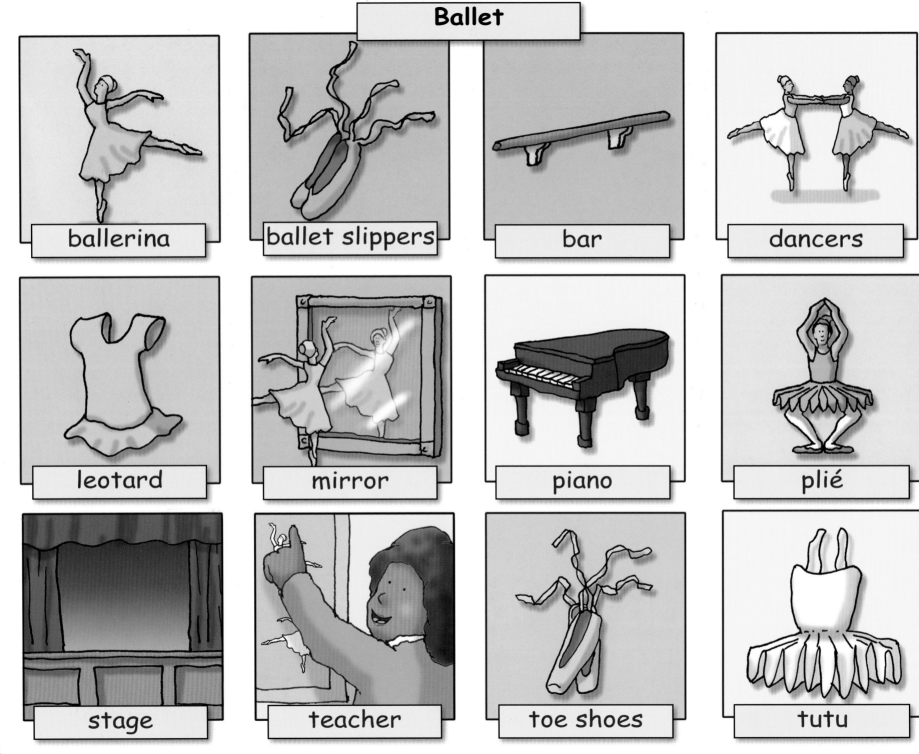

Ballet

ballerina

ballet slippers

bar

dancers

leotard

mirror

piano

plié

stage

teacher

toe shoes

tutu

16

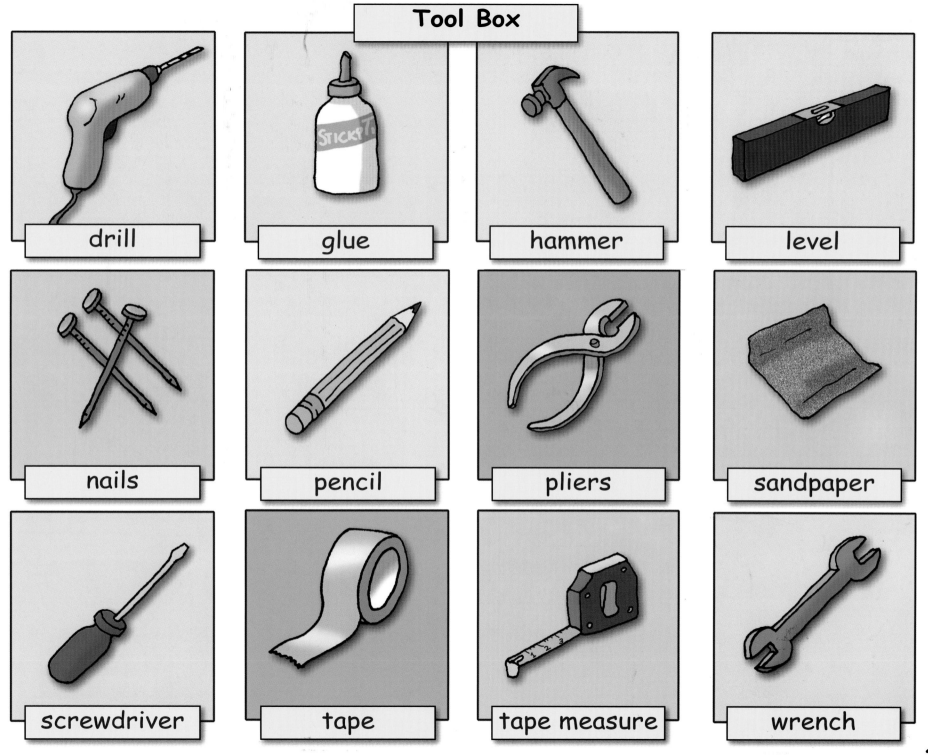

Tool Box

drill

glue

hammer

level

nails

pencil

pliers

sandpaper

screwdriver

tape

tape measure

wrench

17

The Mall

candy store

cash register

coffee shop

escalator

food court

fountain

gum machine

money

movie theater

restaurant

shopping bag

store

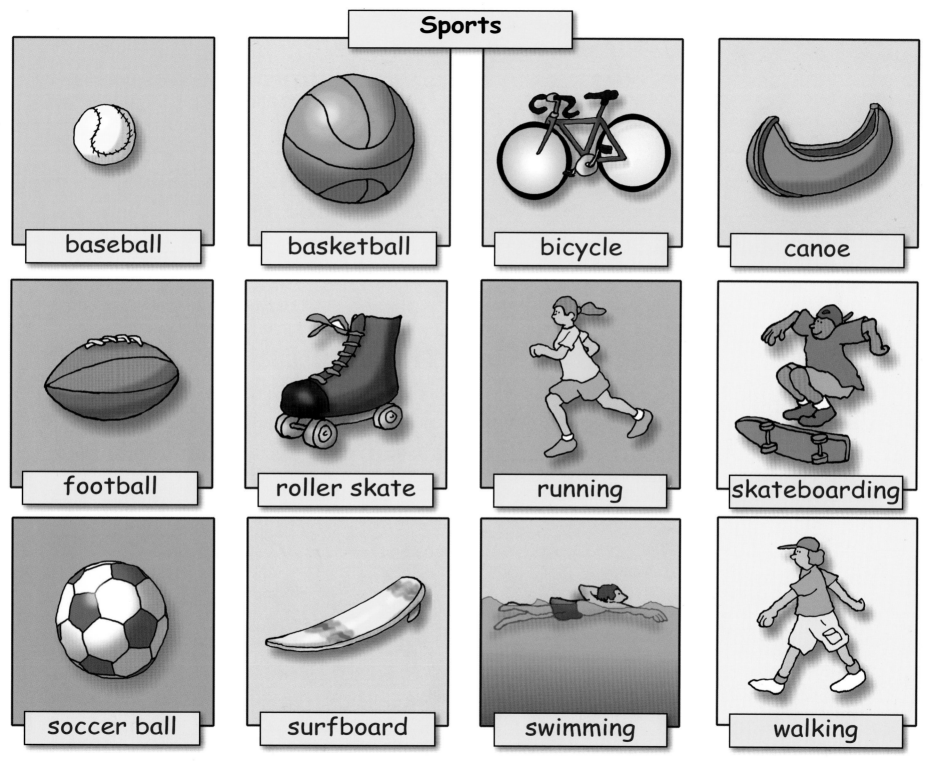

baseball

basketball

bicycle

canoe

football

roller skate

running

skateboarding

soccer ball

surfboard

swimming

walking

The Grocery Store

bags

bologna

bread

butter

cake

candy

cash register

cheese

chips

cookies

crackers

dog food

20

The Grocery Store

eggs

flour

flowers

fruit

mac and cheese

magazines

meat

milk

nuts

seafood

shopping cart

vegetables

21

The Ranch

bandana

bucking bronco

cactus

calf

campfire

cook

cowboy

cowboy hat

coyote

fence

guitar

horse

22

The Ranch

hound dog

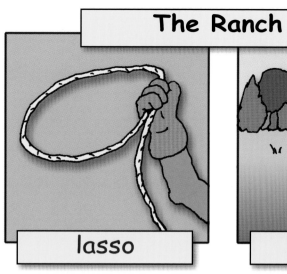
lasso

pasture

pickup truck

rattlesnake

rodeo

rodeo clown

rope

saddle

stampede

steer

wagon

23

The Movie Theater

candy

cartoon

funny

movie

nachos

napkins

popcorn

scary

screen

seat

soda

ticket

24

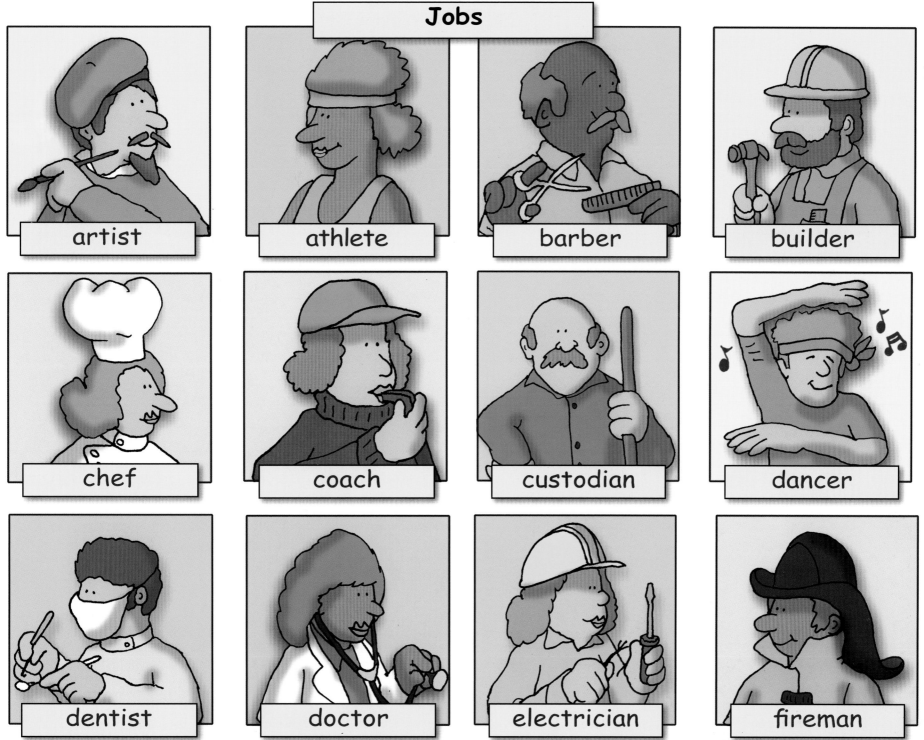

Jobs

artist

athlete

barber

builder

chef

coach

custodian

dancer

dentist

doctor

electrician

fireman

Jobs

fisherman

florist

jeweler

judge

librarian

mail carrier

mayor

mechanic

nurse

painter

paramedic

pastor

Jobs

pilot

plumber

police officer

priest

rabbi

salesman

secretary

server

singer

teacher

trucker

veterinarian

27

Fruits

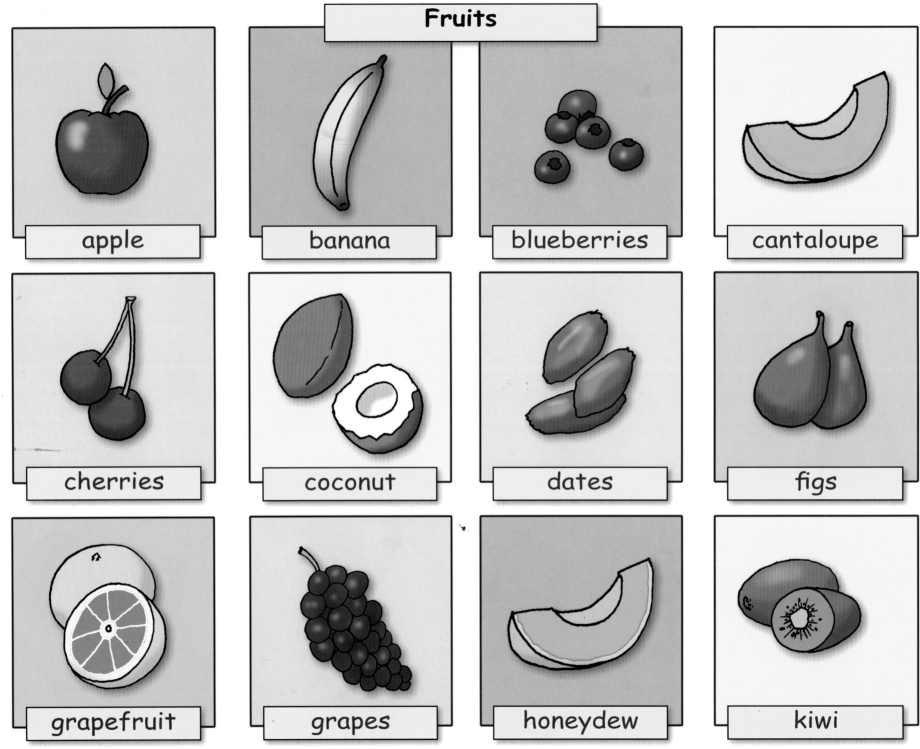

apple

banana

blueberries

cantaloupe

cherries

coconut

dates

figs

grapefruit

grapes

honeydew

kiwi

Fruits

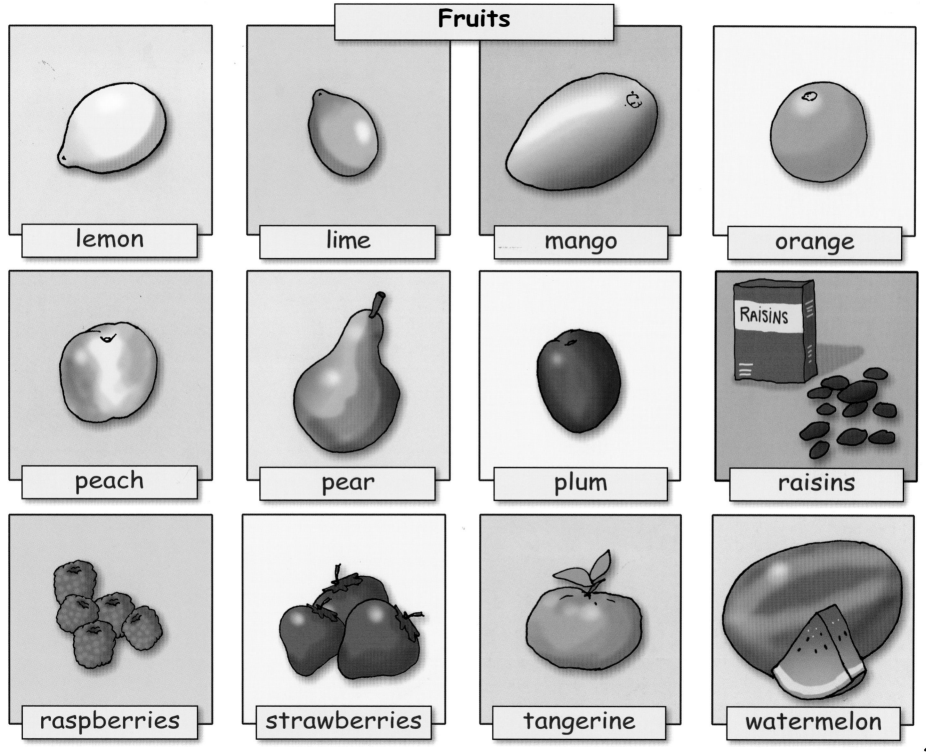

lemon

lime

mango

orange

peach

pear

plum

raisins

RAISINS

raspberries

strawberries

tangerine

watermelon

29

Vegetables

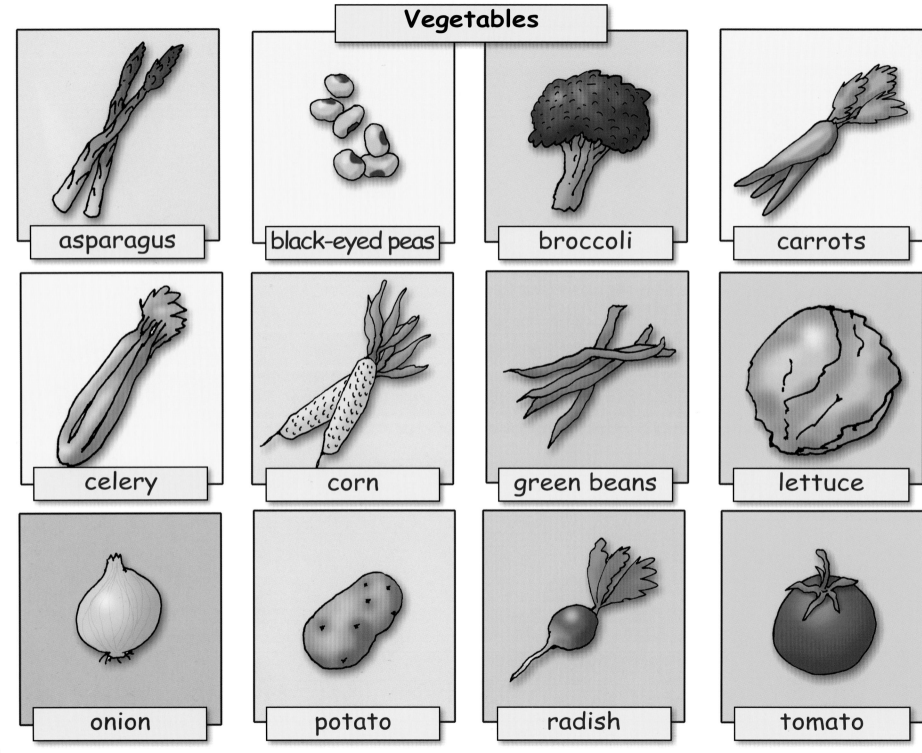

asparagus

black-eyed peas

broccoli

carrots

celery

corn

green beans

lettuce

onion

potato

radish

tomato

30

Snacks

apple

banana

carrots

cereal

cheese & crackers

granola bar

ice cream

juice

milk

popcorn

raisins

veggies & dip

31

Breakfast

bacon

bagel

butter

cereal

chocolate milk

eggs

jelly

juice

milk

oatmeal

toast

tortillas

Supper

baked potato

fried chicken

ham hocks & greens

hot dogs

macaroni & cheese

pizza

pork chop

rice

roast & gravy

salad

spaghetti

steak

33

Camping

bear

campfire

fishing pole

flashlight

ice chest

marshmallows

matches

mosquito

sleeping bag

s'mores

stream

tent

34

Months of the Year

January

February

March

April

May

June

July

August

September

October

November

December

35

Buildings

bakery

bank

barbershop

courthouse

garage

gas station

grocery store

hospital

hotel

post office

restaurant

school

36

Weather

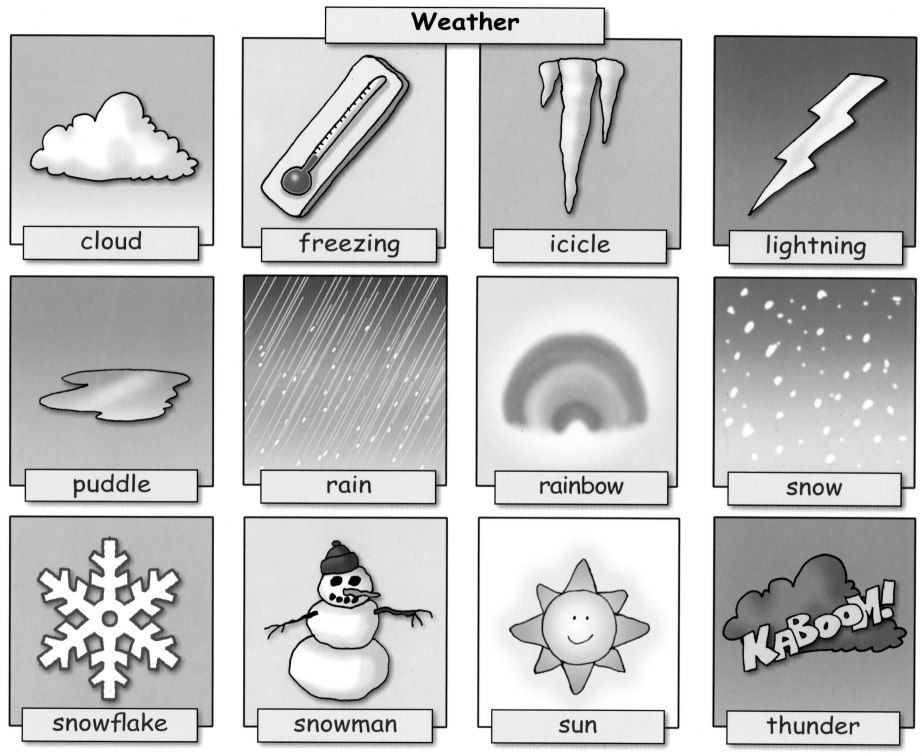

cloud

freezing

icicle

lightning

puddle

rain

rainbow

snow

snowflake

snowman

sun

thunder

37

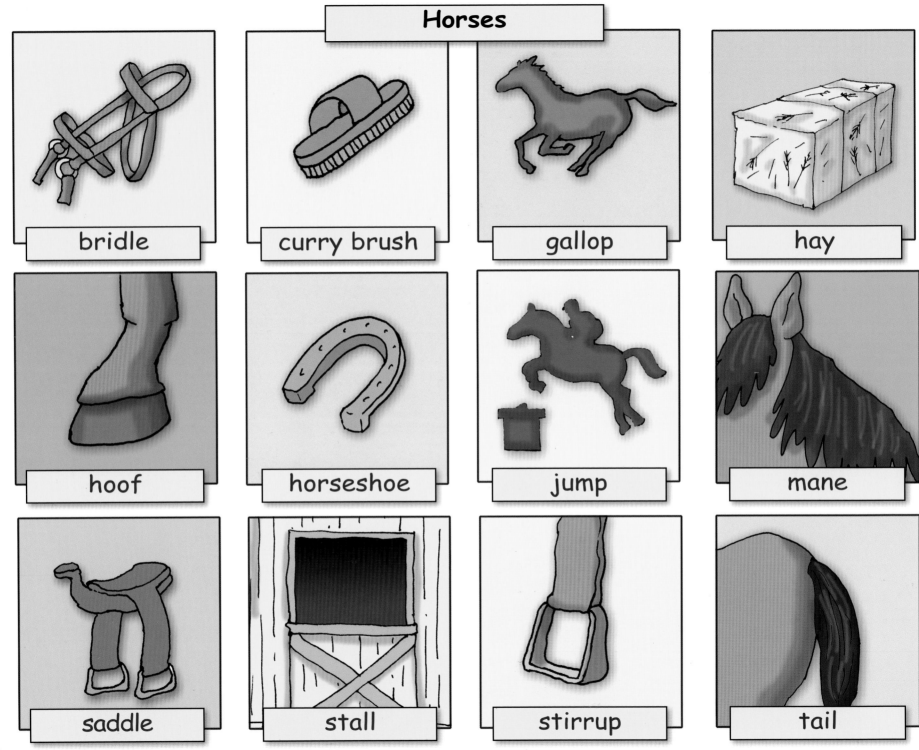

Horses

bridle

curry brush

gallop

hay

hoof

horseshoe

jump

mane

saddle

stall

stirrup

tail

The Birthday Party

balloons

cake

camera

friends

hats

ice cream

invitation

party favors

piñata

pin-the-tail-on-the-donkey

presents

video camera

39

Fishing

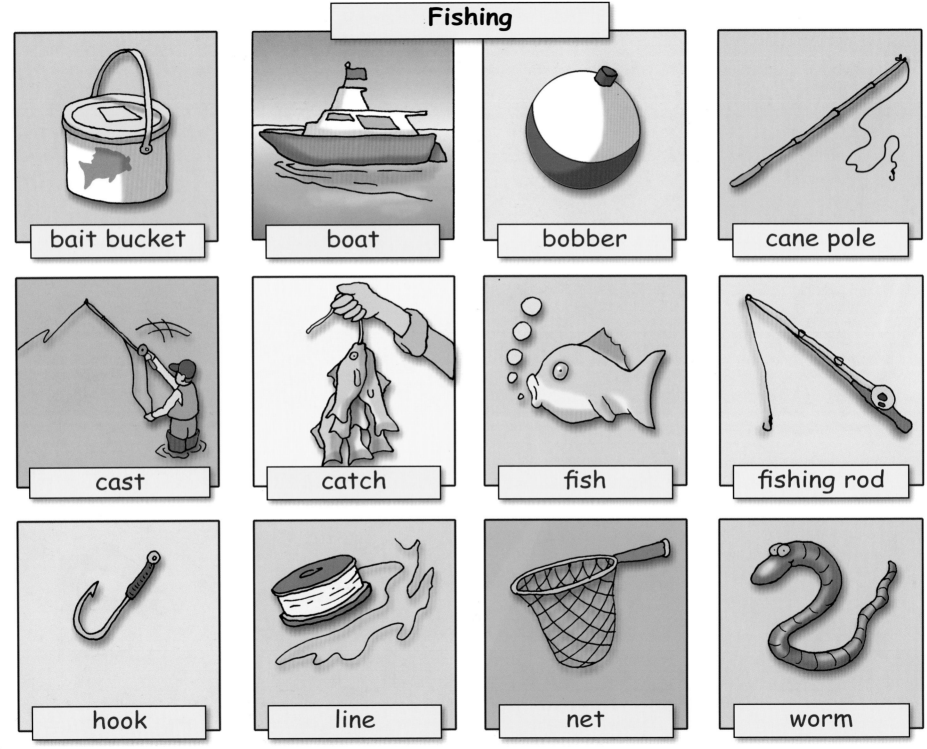

bait bucket

boat

bobber

cane pole

cast

catch

fish

fishing rod

hook

line

net

worm

40

The Pool

dive

diving board

float

goggles

jump

kick

ladder

lifeguard

pool toys

splash

swim

water

apron

batter

beaters

bowl

brownies

brown sugar

butter

cake

chocolate chips

cookies

cookie sheet

flour

42

Cooking

frying pan

hot mitt

measuring cup

mixer

oven

sink

spoon

stove

sugar

timer

wash the dishes

whisk

43

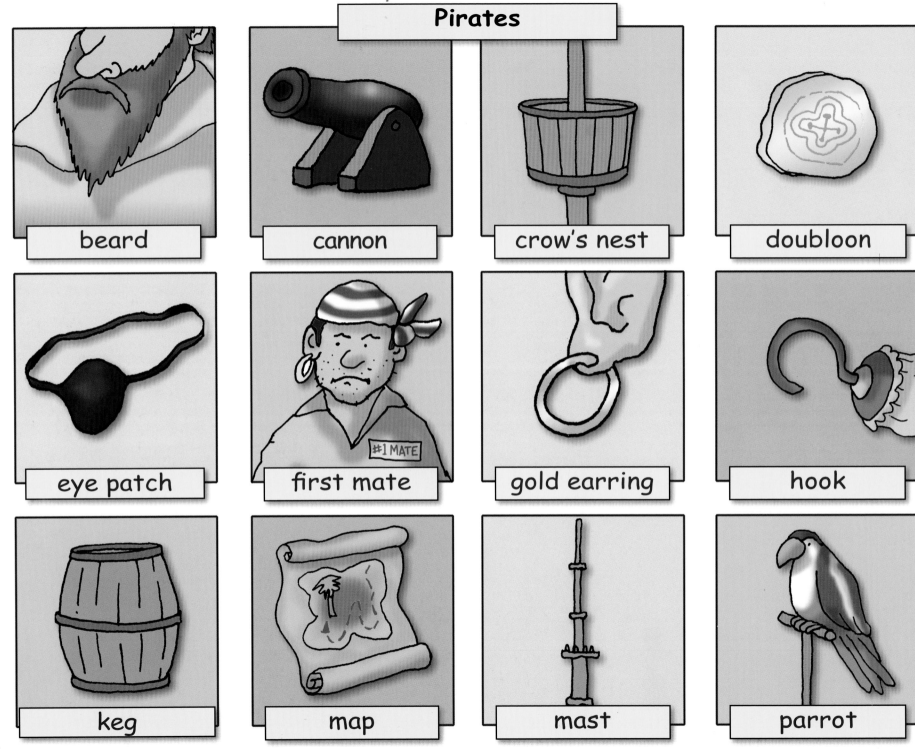

Pirates

beard

cannon

crow's nest

doubloon

eye patch

first mate

#1 MATE

gold earring

hook

keg

map

mast

parrot

44

Pirates

pirate

pirate ship

plank

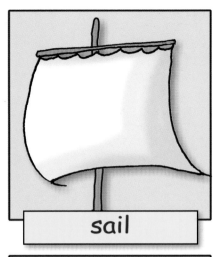
sail

skull & crossbones

spyglass

swabbing the deck

sword

treasure

wheel

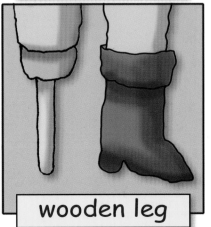
wooden leg

X marks the spot

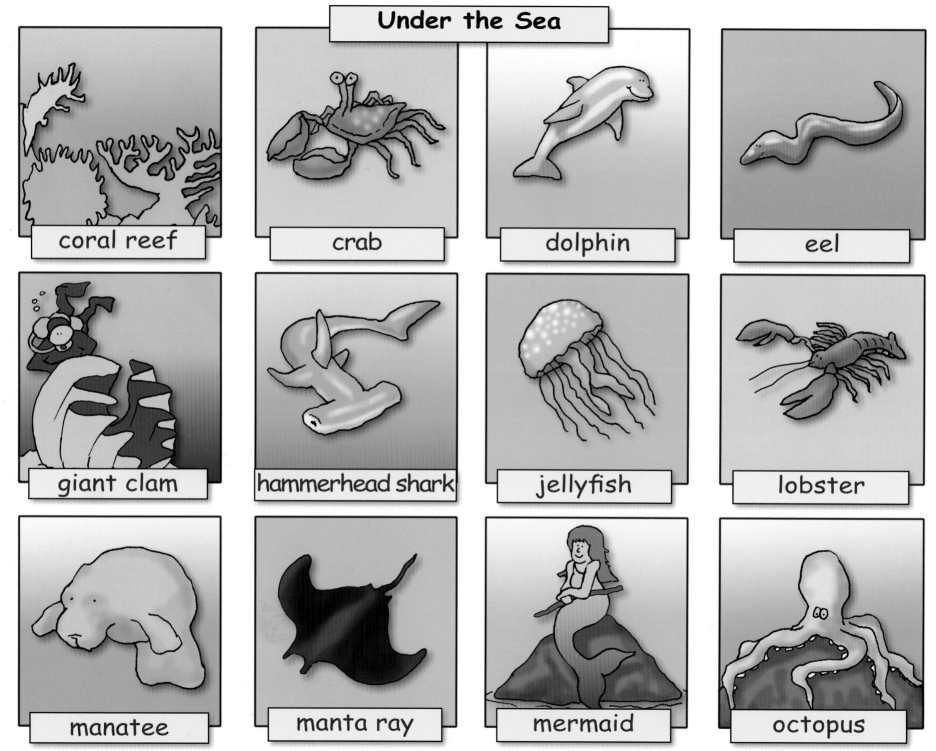

Under the Sea

coral reef

crab

dolphin

eel

giant clam

hammerhead shark

jellyfish

lobster

manatee

manta ray

mermaid

octopus

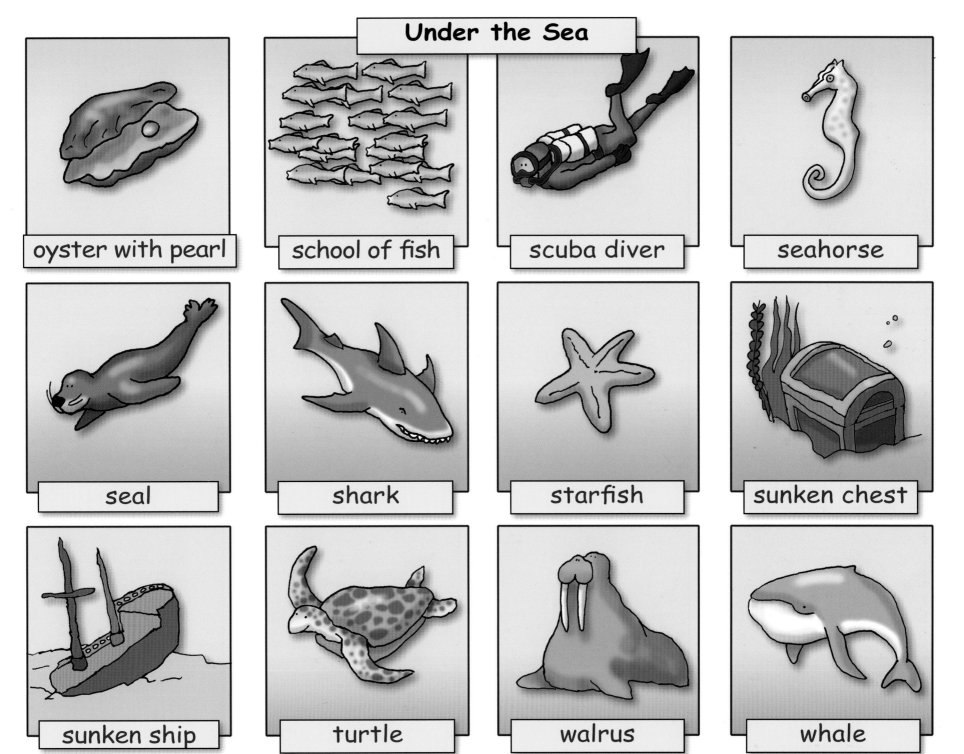

Under the Sea

oyster with pearl

school of fish

scuba diver

seahorse

seal

shark

starfish

sunken chest

sunken ship

turtle

walrus

whale

47

Pets

bird

cat

dog

ferret

goldfish

hamster

horse

iguana

kitten

mouse

pot-bellied pig

puppy

48

Chores

bring in the mail

change the kitty litter

dry the dishes

dust the furniture

make my bed

pick up my toys

sweep the floor

take out the garbage

walk the dog

wash the dishes

water the flowers

wipe the table

49

Medieval Fantasy

bow and arrow

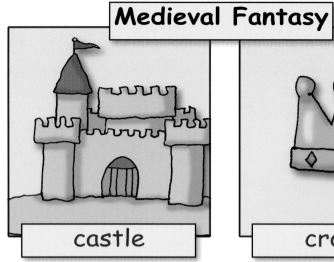
castle

crown

dragon

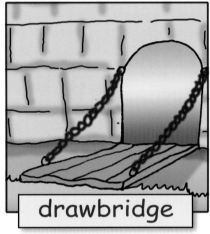
drawbridge

dungeon

enchanted forest

giant

guard

king

knight-in-shining armor

magic spell

Medieval Fantasy

magic wand

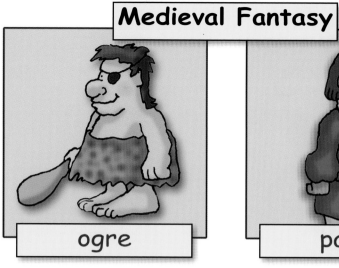
ogre

page

prince

princess

queen

suit of armor

sword

throne

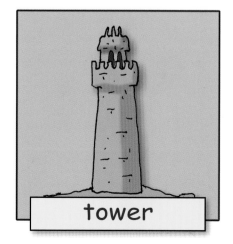
tower

troll

wizard

51

build a fort

call someone on the phone

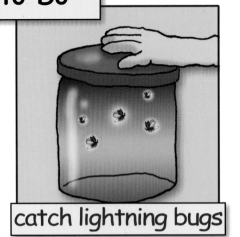
catch lightning bugs

climb a tree

count my money

decorate my room

dress up in funny clothes

e-mail my friend

feed the birds

float in the pool

fly a kite

go fishing

52

Things to Do

go for a walk

jump rope

kick the ball

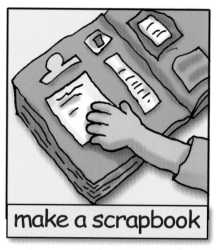
make a scrapbook

paint a picture

plant a garden

play video games

practice the piano

put on a puppet show

put together a puzzle

read a good book

relax in the hammock

Things to Do

ride my bike

ride on my razor scooter

rollerblade

shoot hoops

sit in my tree house

skateboard

swing high

take pictures

visit my neighbor

wade in the creek

watch t.v.

write a letter

Goldilocks and the Three Bears

Baby Bear

bed

bowl

chair

cottage

Goldilocks

Mama Bear

Papa Bear

porridge

spoon

upstairs

woods

55

Little Red Riding Hood

basket of goodies

bed

Big Bad Wolf

big eyes

big nose

big teeth

grandmother

grandmother's house

Little Red Riding Hood

path

woods

woodsman

Jack and the Beanstalk

beanstalk

castle

cottage

cow

giant

golden egg

golden harp

goose

Jack

magic beans

mother

sack of gold

Make-Believe Story Words

billy goats

bridge

broomstick

coach

elf

fairy

fairy godmother

frog

genie

genie's lamp

glass slipper

leprechaun

58

Make-Believe Story Words

magic carpet

magic wand

mermaid

mirror on the wall

poison apple

potion

prince

princess

pumpkin

swan

troll

witch

59

The Three Little Pigs

Big Bad Wolf

blow your house down

bricks

chimney

fire

house

huff and puff

kettle

straw

three little pigs

wheelbarrow

wood

60

The Hospital

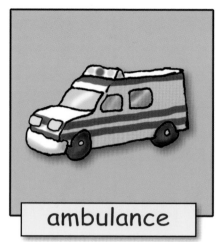
ambulance

doctor

emergency room

newborn nursery

nurse

paramedic

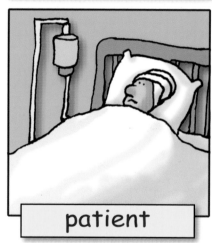
patient

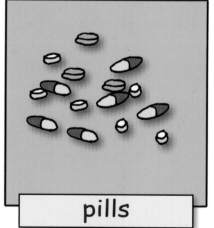
pills

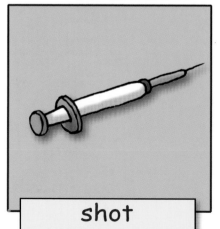
shot

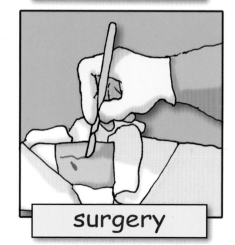
surgery

waiting room

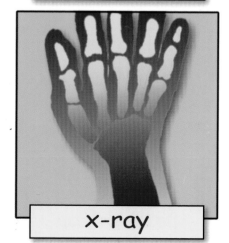
x-ray

The Fair

4-H

beauty queen

blue ribbon

bumper car

candy apple

corn dog

cotton candy

Ferris wheel

first prize

funnelcake

hot dog

judge

62

The Fair

merry-go-round

pie-eating contest

pony ride

popcorn

prizes

quilt

sheep

shooting gallery

soda

stuffed animals

swing

tractor

Grooming

braid my hair

brush my teeth

clean my ears

comb my hair

floss my teeth

powder my body

scrub my body

shampoo my hair

shower

take a bath

trim my nails

wash my hands

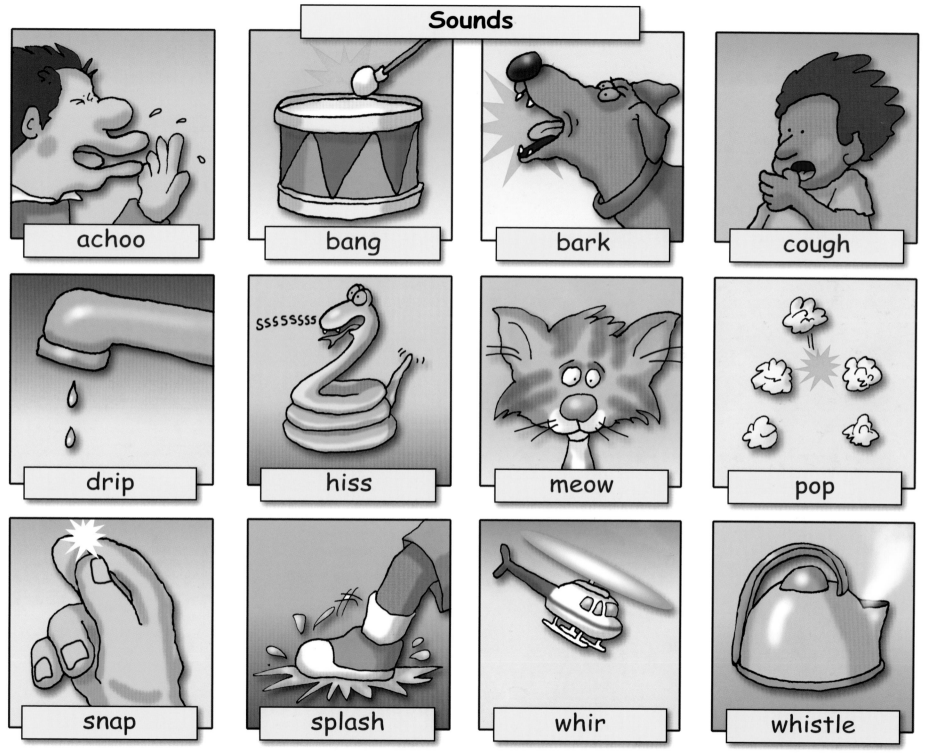

65

The Candy Store

bubble gum

candy case

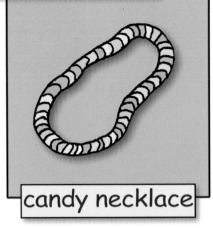
candy necklace

caramel

chocolate bar

fudge

jawbreaker

jelly beans

licorice

lollipops

peanut butter cups

taffy

66

The Countryside

beehive

bird's nest

bright stars

buggy

covered bridge

cricket

frog

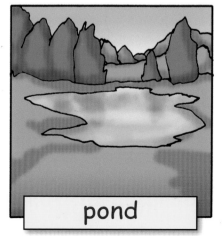

geese

lily pad

meadow

pond

wagon

The Orchestra

bass

bass drum

bassoon

baton

cello

clarinet

conductor

flute

French horn

marimba

music stand

oboe

68

The Orchestra

piano

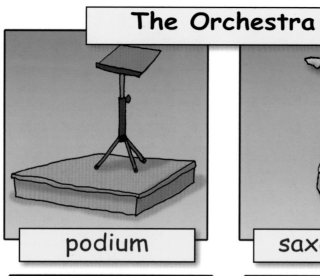
podium

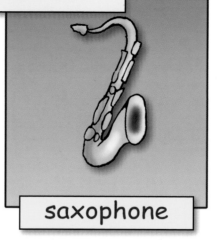
saxophone

score

snare drum

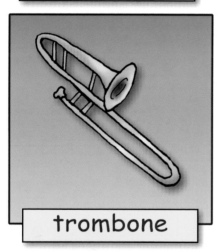
trombone

trumpet

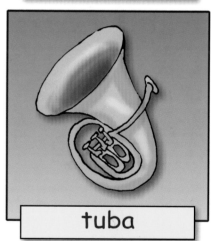
tuba

tympani

viola

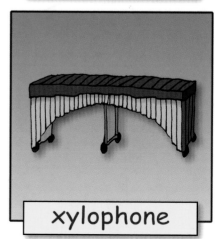
violin

xylophone

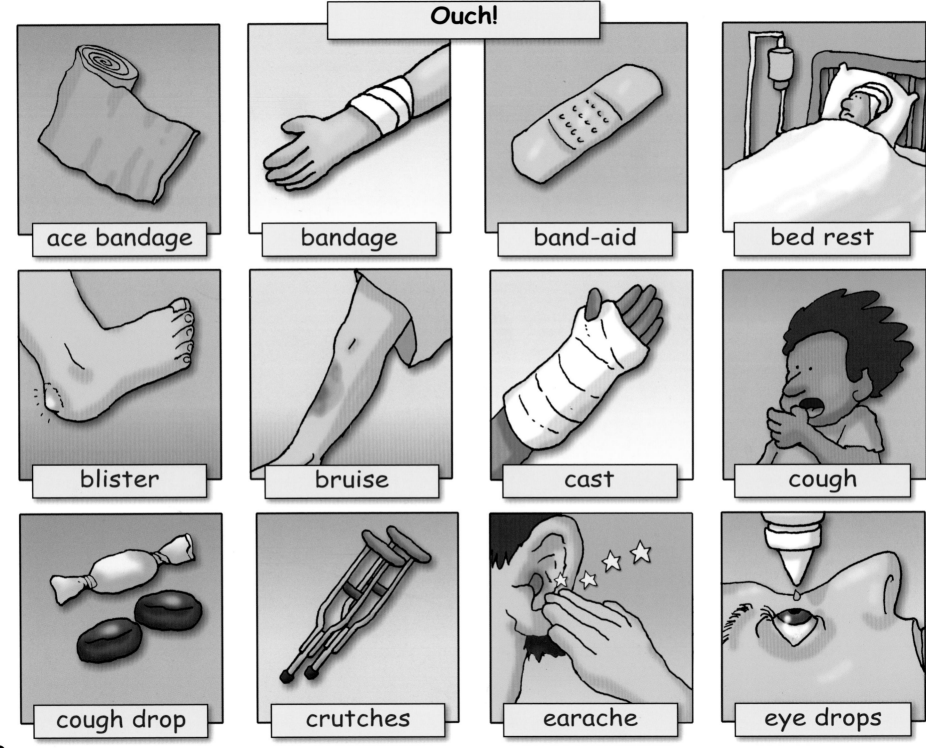

Ouch!

ace bandage

bandage

band-aid

bed rest

blister

bruise

cast

cough

cough drop

crutches

earache

eye drops

70

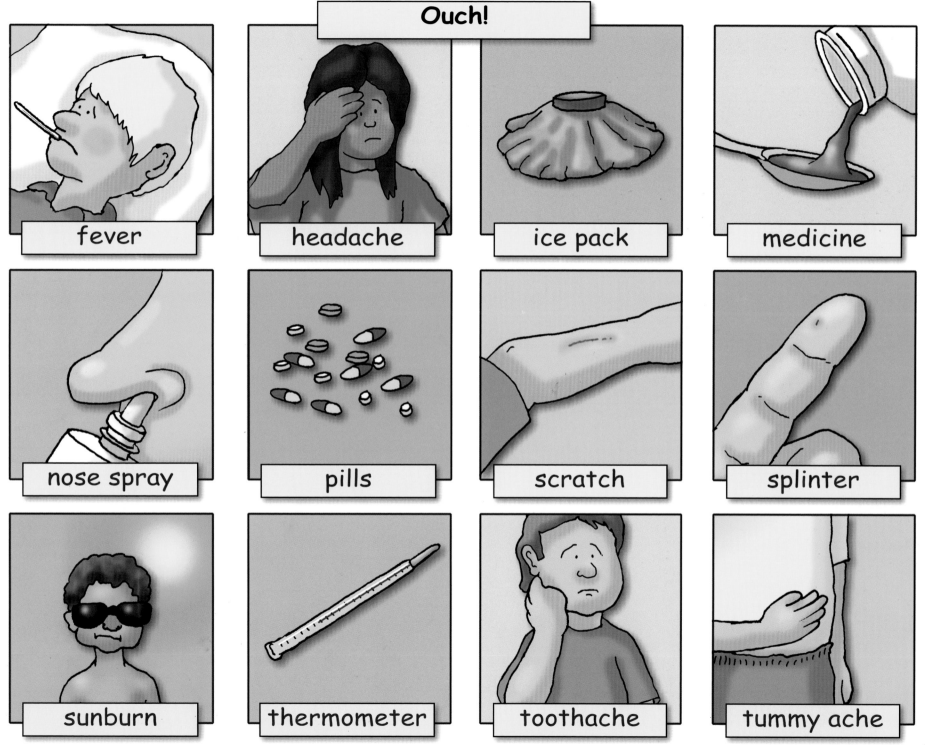

Ouch!

fever

headache

ice pack

medicine

nose spray

pills

scratch

splinter

sunburn

thermometer

toothache

tummy ache

71

Wheels

18 wheeler

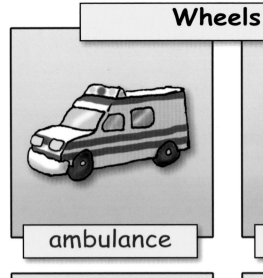

ambulance

bus

cement truck

dump truck

fire truck

garbage truck

jeep

monster truck

motorcycle

pickup truck

race car

72

Parade

balloon

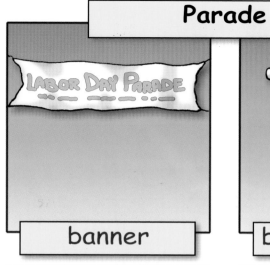
banner

baton twirler

beauty queen

clown

crowd

drum major

fire truck

float

majorette

marching band

mayor

73

Wrestling

announcer

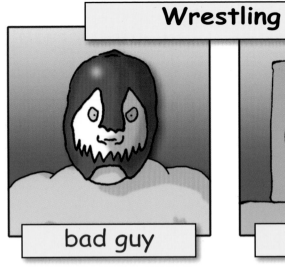
bad guy

bell

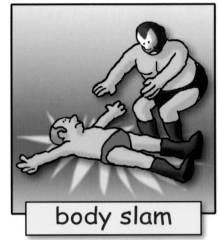
body slam

champion belt

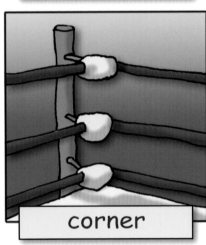
corner

good guy

headlock

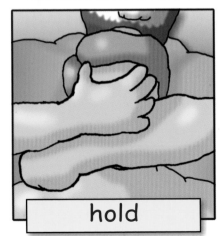
hold

ref

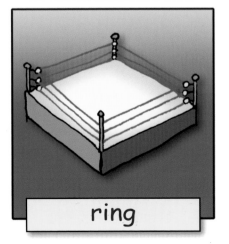
ring

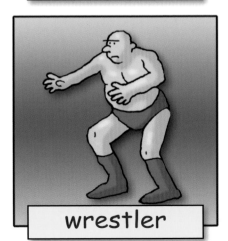
wrestler

74

Money

allowance

bank

change

dime

dollar

fifty-cent piece

nickel

penny

piggy bank

quarter

savings book

teller

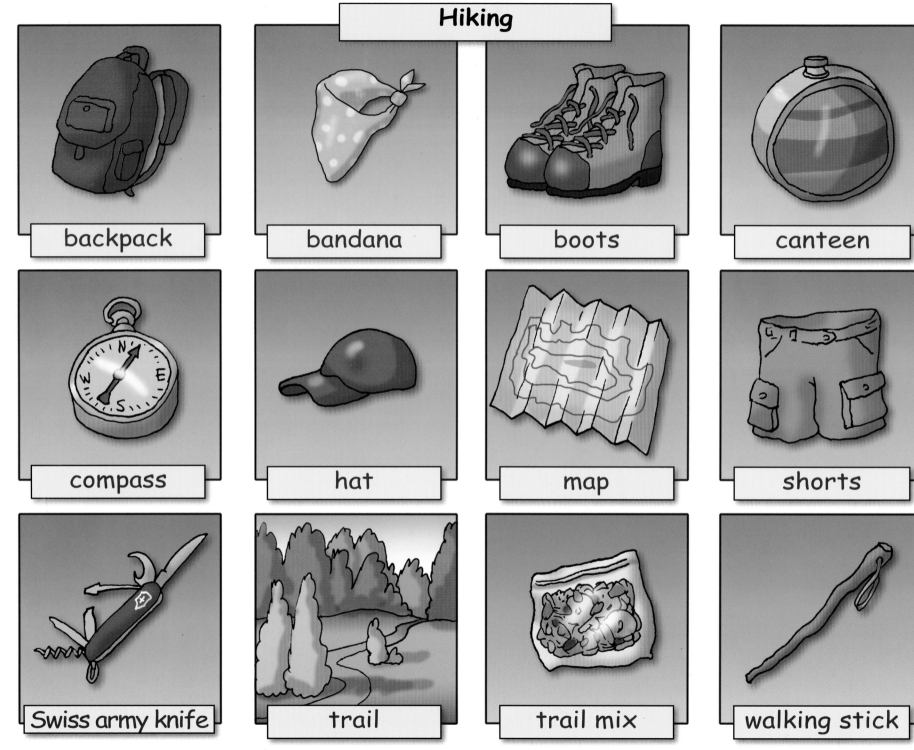

Hiking

backpack

bandana

boots

canteen

compass

hat

map

shorts

Swiss army knife

trail

trail mix

walking stick

76

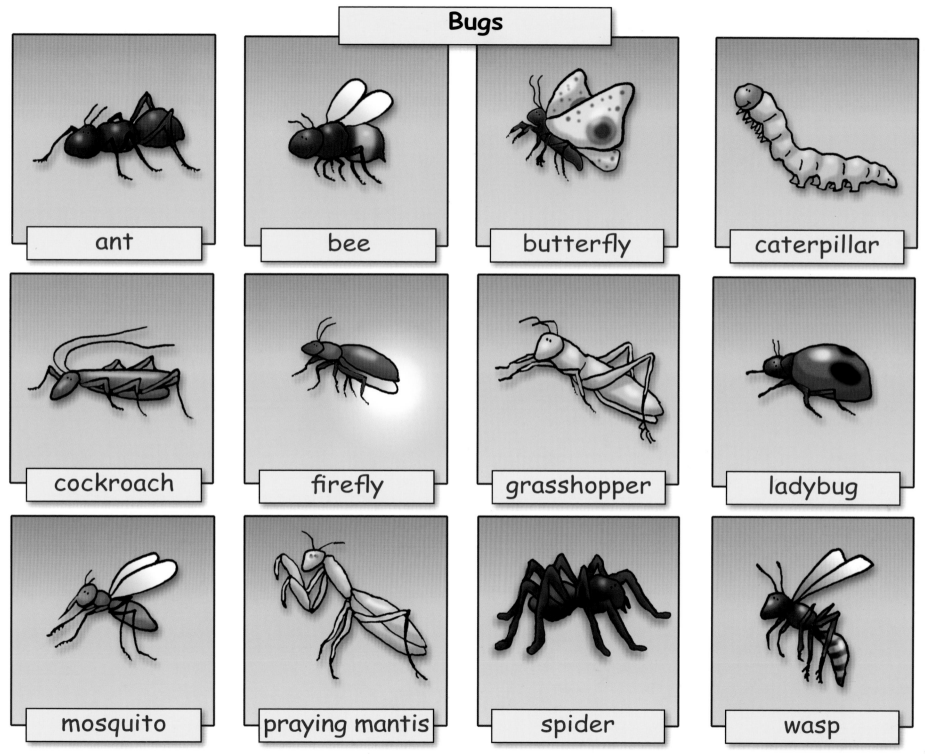

Bugs

ant

bee

butterfly

caterpillar

cockroach

firefly

grasshopper

ladybug

mosquito

praying mantis

spider

wasp

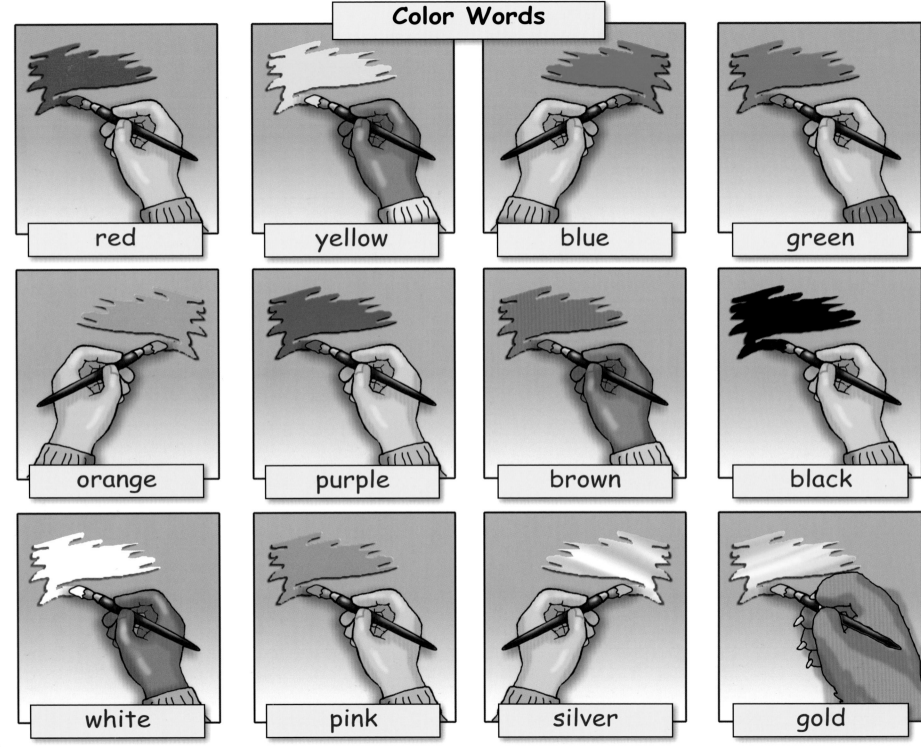

Color Words

red

yellow

blue

green

orange

purple

brown

black

white

pink

silver

gold

78

Polar Animals

arctic fox

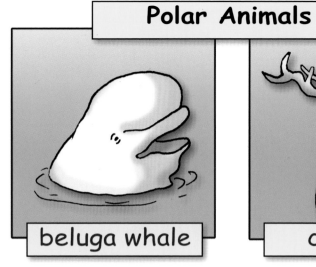
beluga whale

caribou

killer whale

narwhal

penguin

polar bear

reindeer

seal

sled dog

snowy owl

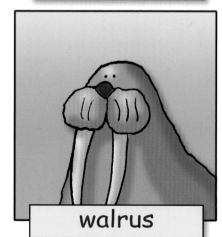
walrus

79

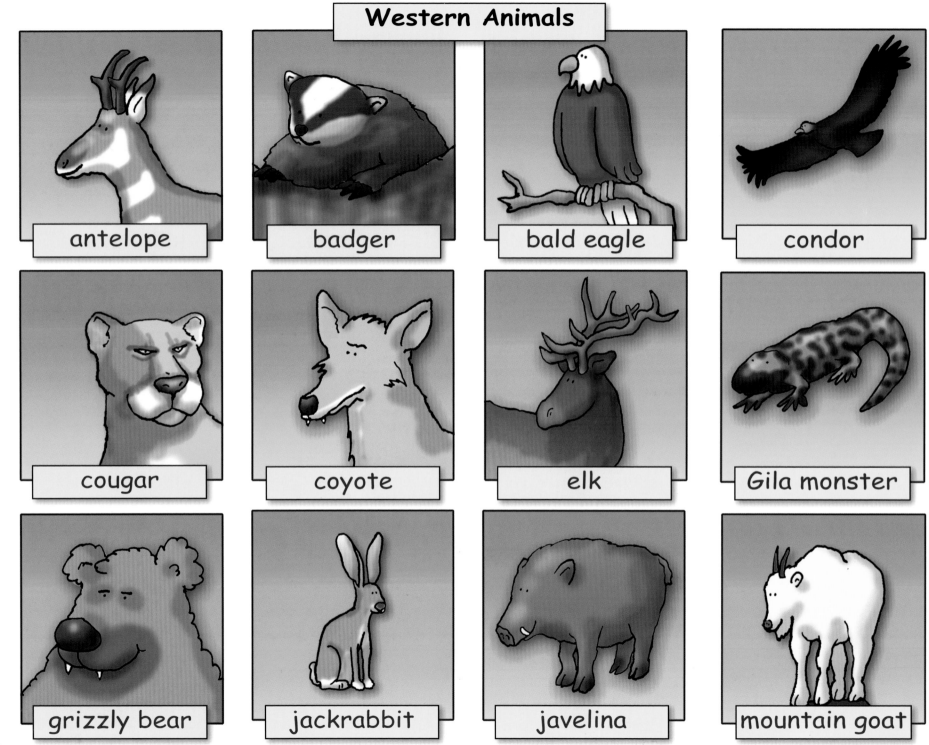

Western Animals

antelope

badger

bald eagle

condor

cougar

coyote

elk

Gila monster

grizzly bear

jackrabbit

javelina

mountain goat

Western Animals

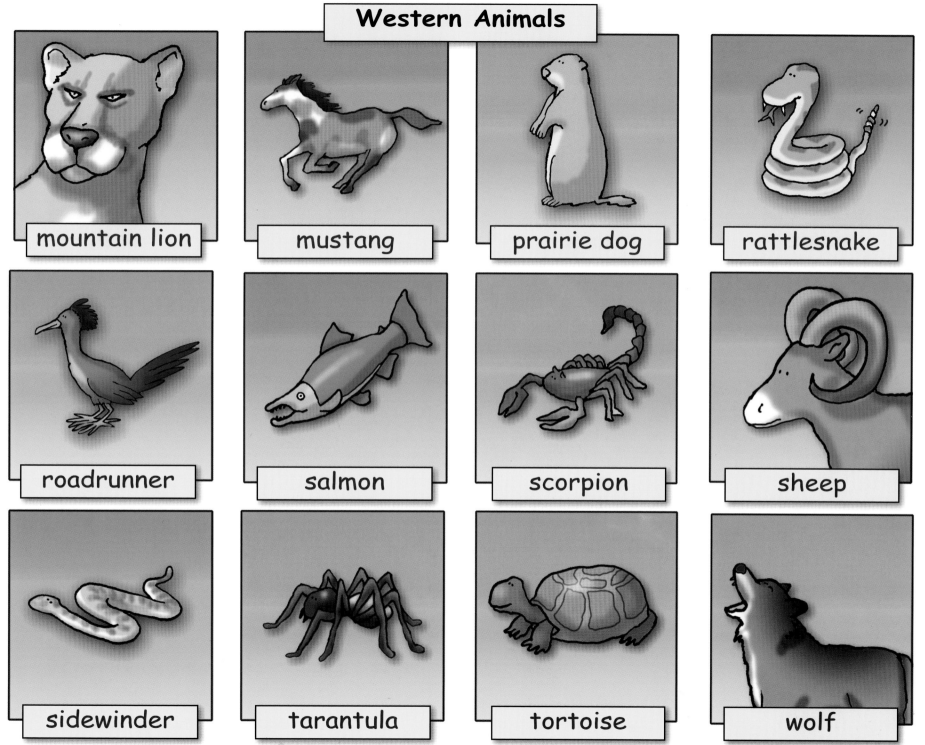

mountain lion

mustang

prairie dog

rattlesnake

roadrunner

salmon

scorpion

sheep

sidewinder

tarantula

tortoise

wolf

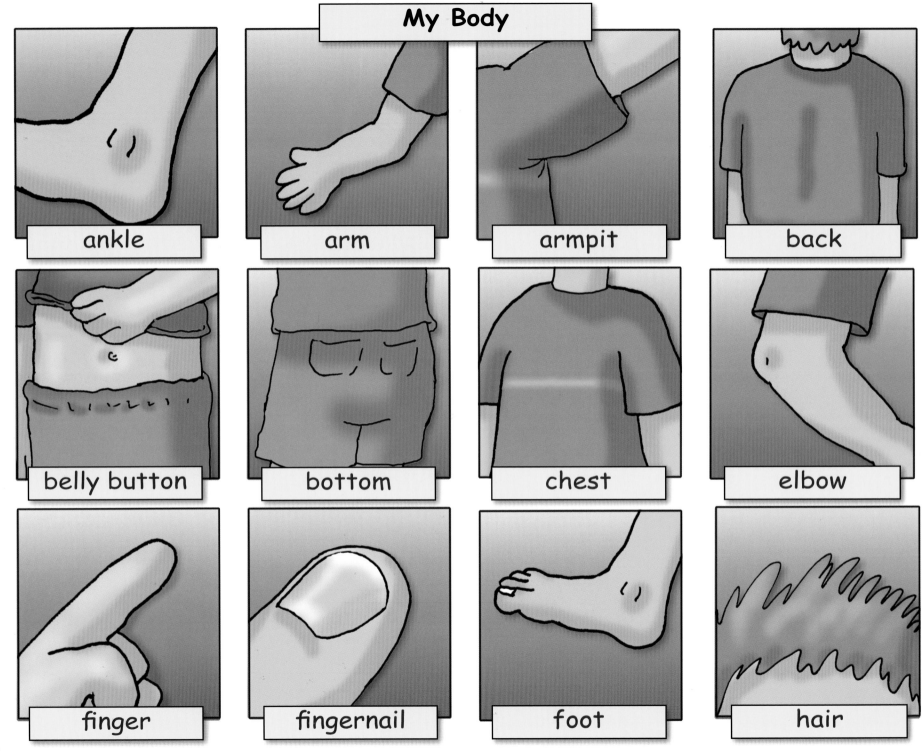

My Body

ankle

arm

armpit

back

belly button

bottom

chest

elbow

finger

fingernail

foot

hair

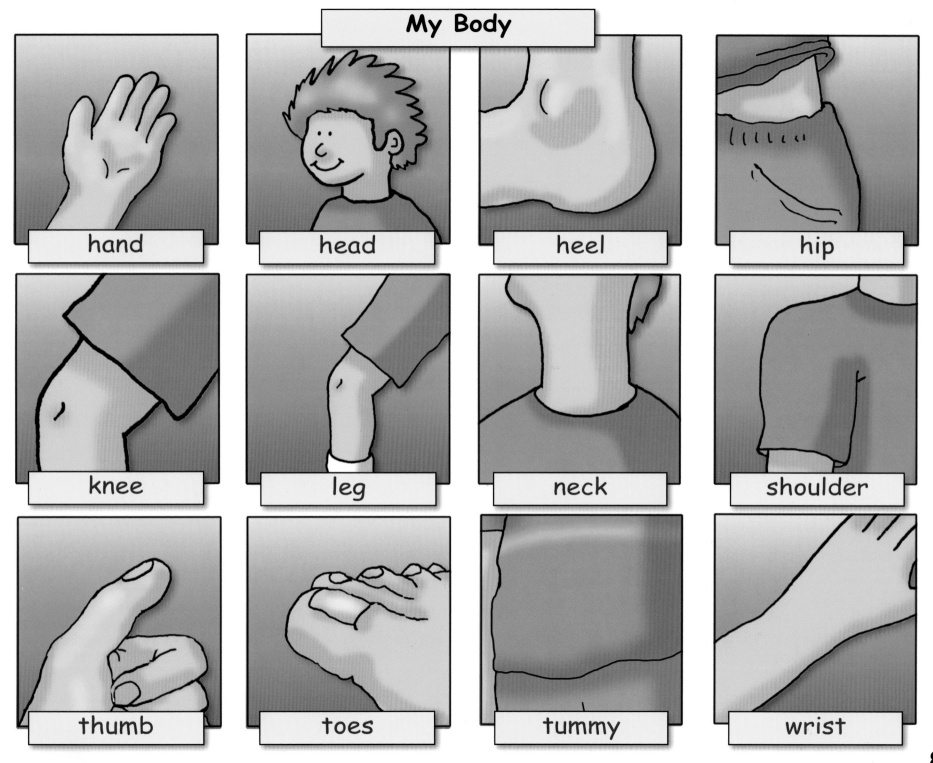

My Body

hand

head

heel

hip

knee

leg

neck

shoulder

thumb

toes

tummy

wrist

83

Computer Words

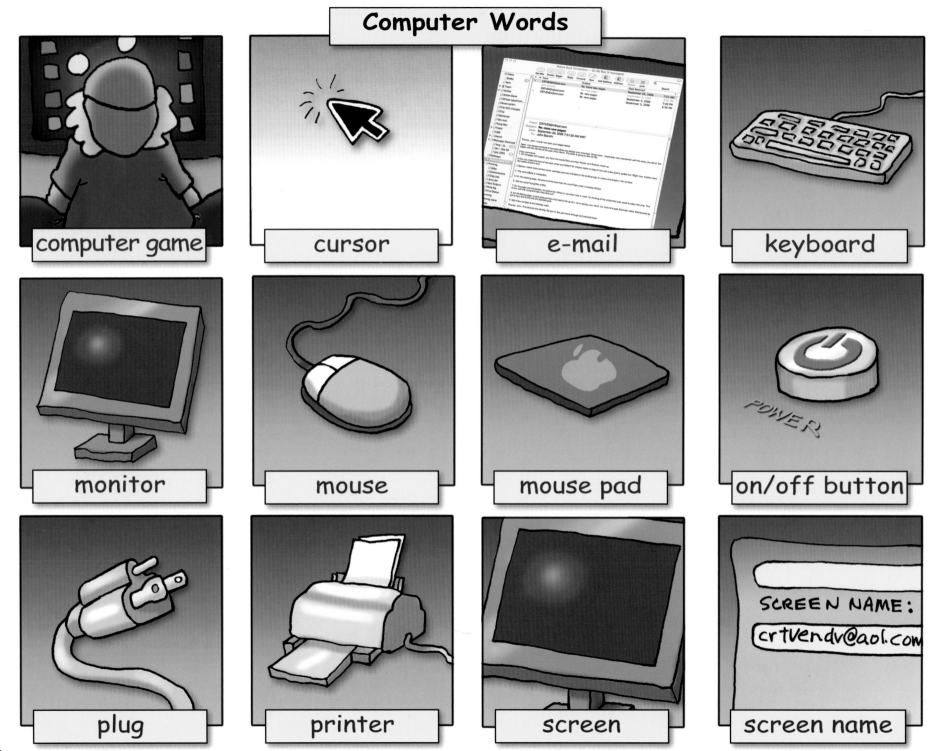

computer game

cursor

e-mail

keyboard

monitor

mouse

mouse pad

on/off button

POWER

plug

printer

screen

screen name

SCREEN NAME:
crtvendv@aol.com

84

Family

mother

father

sister

brother

baby

grandmother

grandfather

twins

teenager

toddler

family photo

dog

85

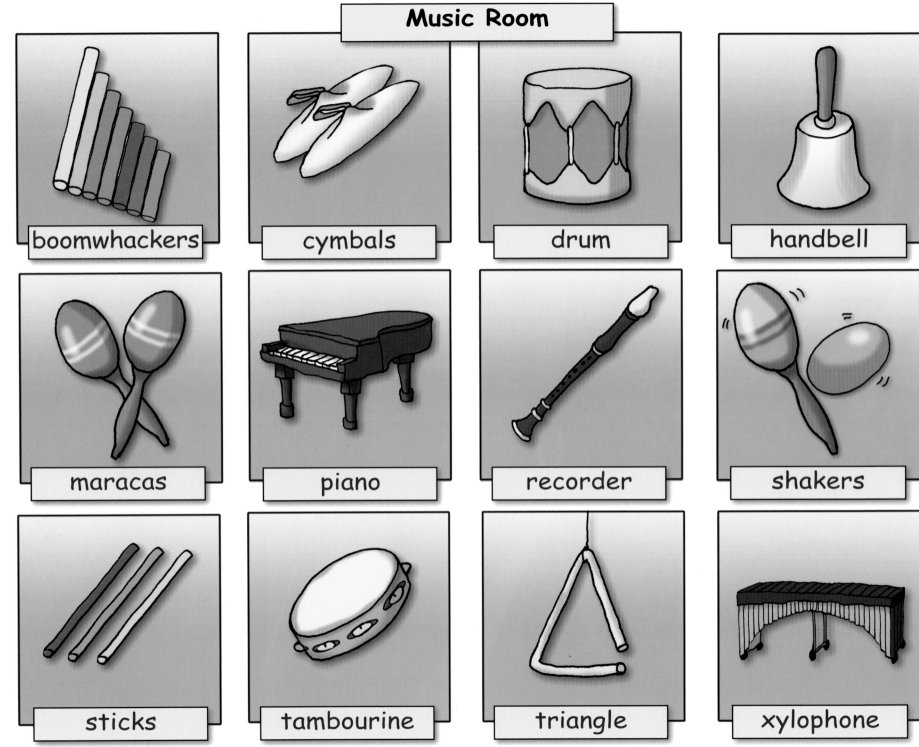

boomwhackers

cymbals

drum

handbell

maracas

piano

recorder

shakers

sticks

tambourine

triangle

xylophone

Lunch

carrots

fruit

hamburger

juice box

lunchbox

milk

pizza

pretzel

pudding

sandwich

soup

string cheese

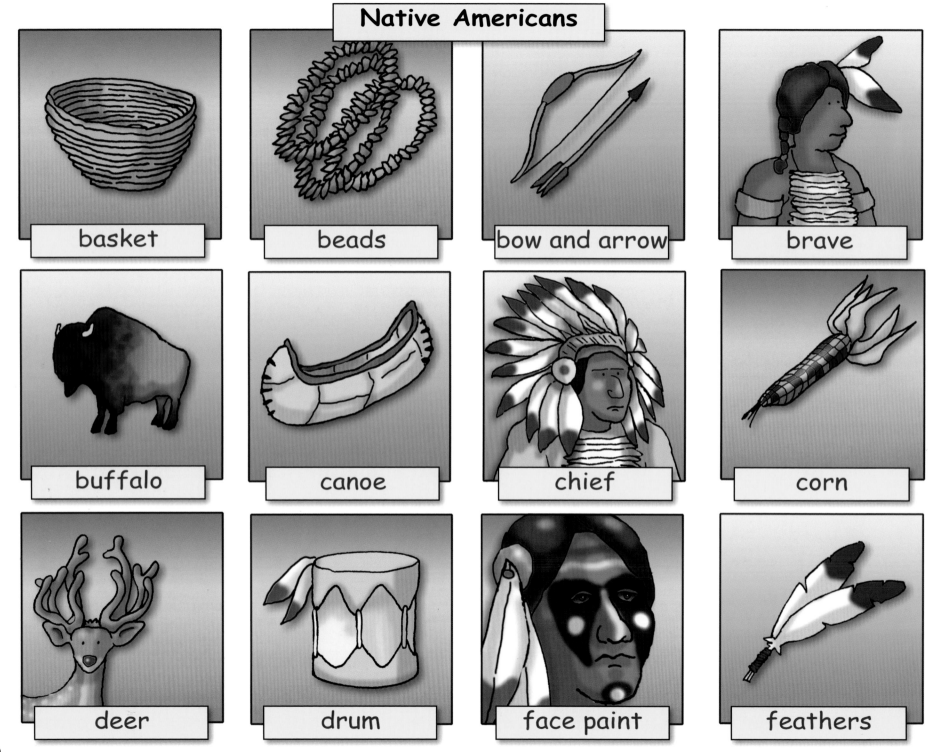

Native Americans

basket

beads

bow and arrow

brave

buffalo

canoe

chief

corn

deer

drum

face paint

feathers

Native Americans

fire

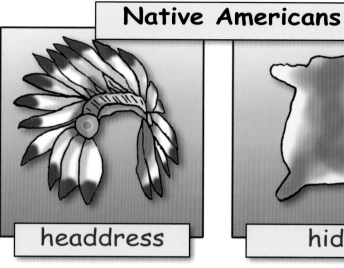
headdress

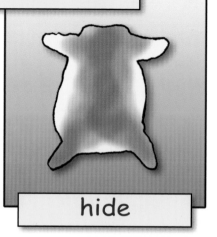
hide

moccasins

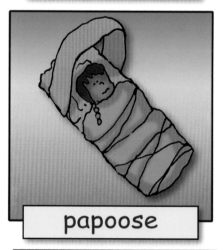
papoose

pinto

raindance

smoke signal

spear

tepee

tomahawk

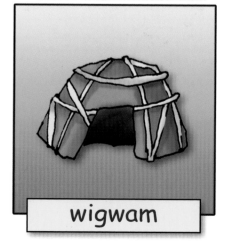
wigwam

89

American Inuits

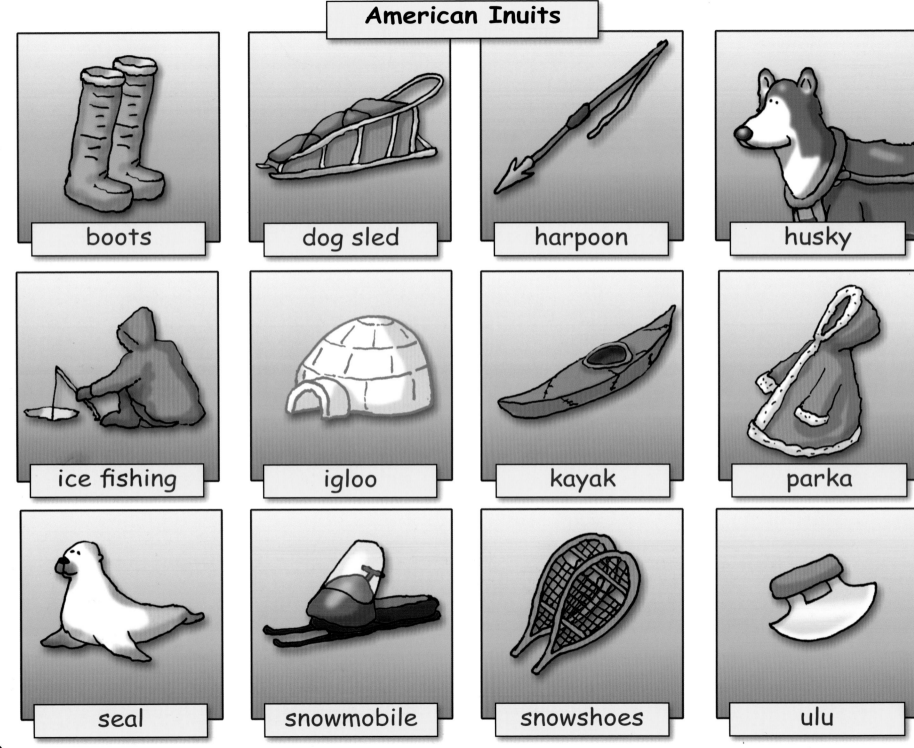

boots

dog sled

harpoon

husky

ice fishing

igloo

kayak

parka

seal

snowmobile

snowshoes

ulu

Thanksgiving

blessing

corn

cranberries

feast

football

harvest

Mayflower

Native American

pilgrims

pumpkin

pumpkin pie

turkey

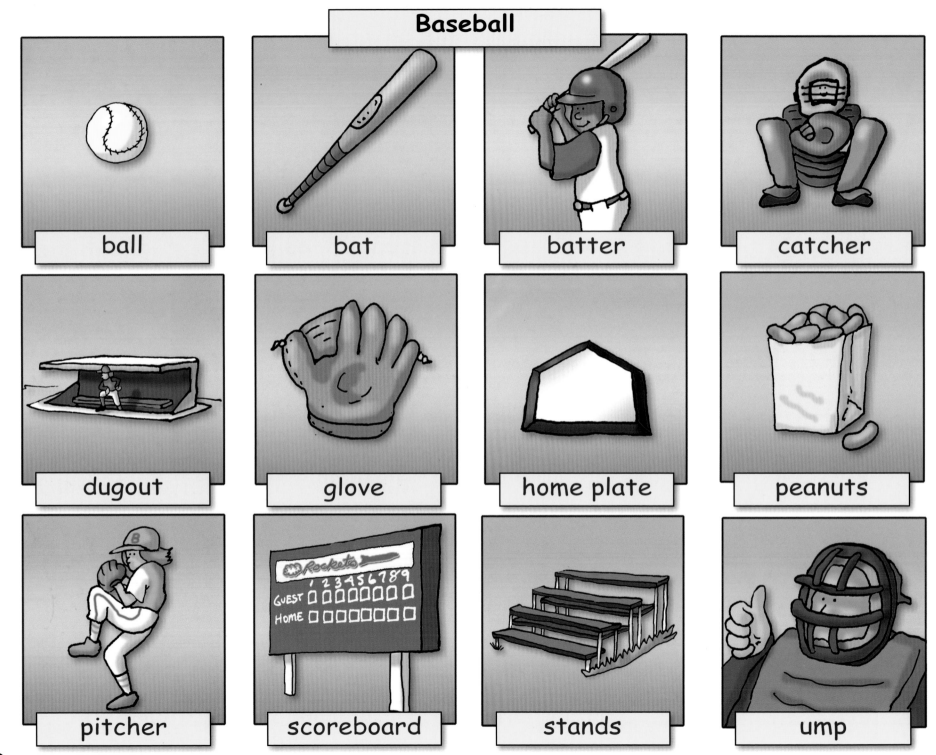

Baseball

ball

bat

batter

catcher

dugout

glove

home plate

peanuts

pitcher

scoreboard

stands

ump

Reptiles

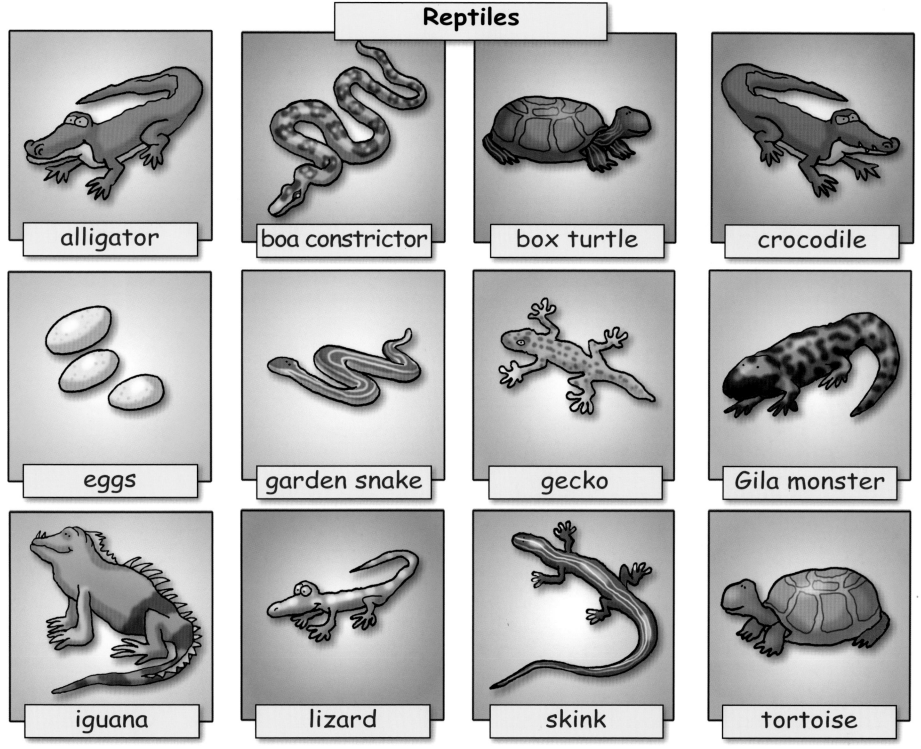

alligator

boa constrictor

box turtle

crocodile

eggs

garden snake

gecko

Gila monster

iguana

lizard

skink

tortoise

Holidays

New Year's Day

Dr. Martin Luther King Day

Valentine's Day

St. Patrick's Day

Easter

4th of July

Yom Kippur

Veterans Day

Thanksgiving

Hannukah

Christmas

Kwanzaa

Basketball

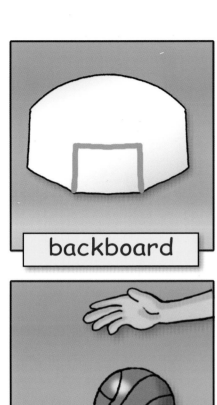
backboard

basketball

cheerleader

coach

dribble

hightops

hoop

jersey

jump

net

scoreboard

whistle

95

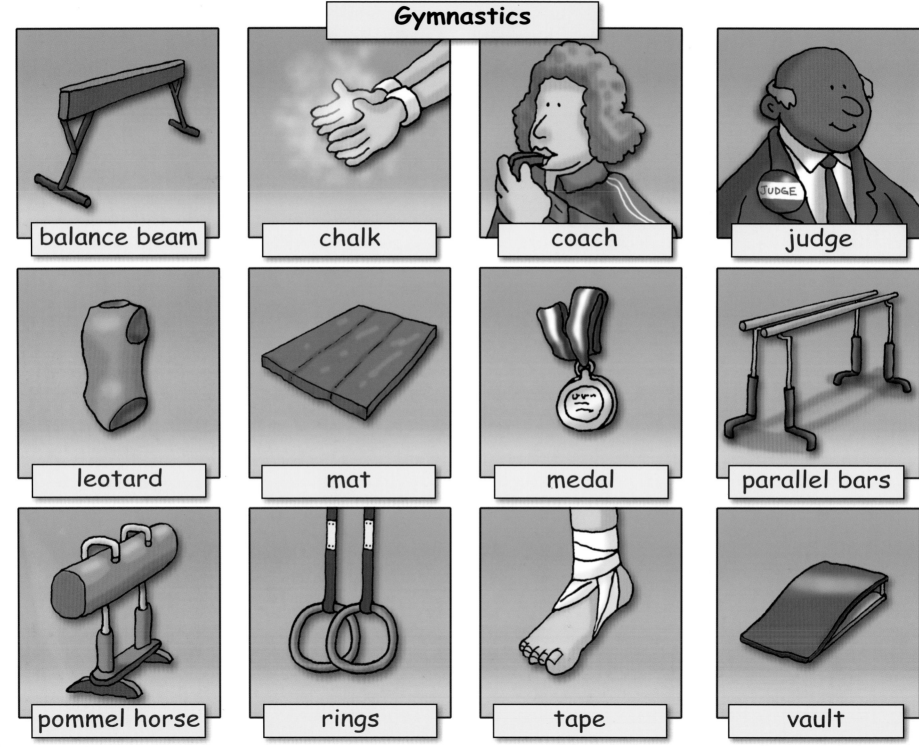

Gymnastics

balance beam

chalk

coach

judge

leotard

mat

medal

parallel bars

pommel horse

rings

tape

vault

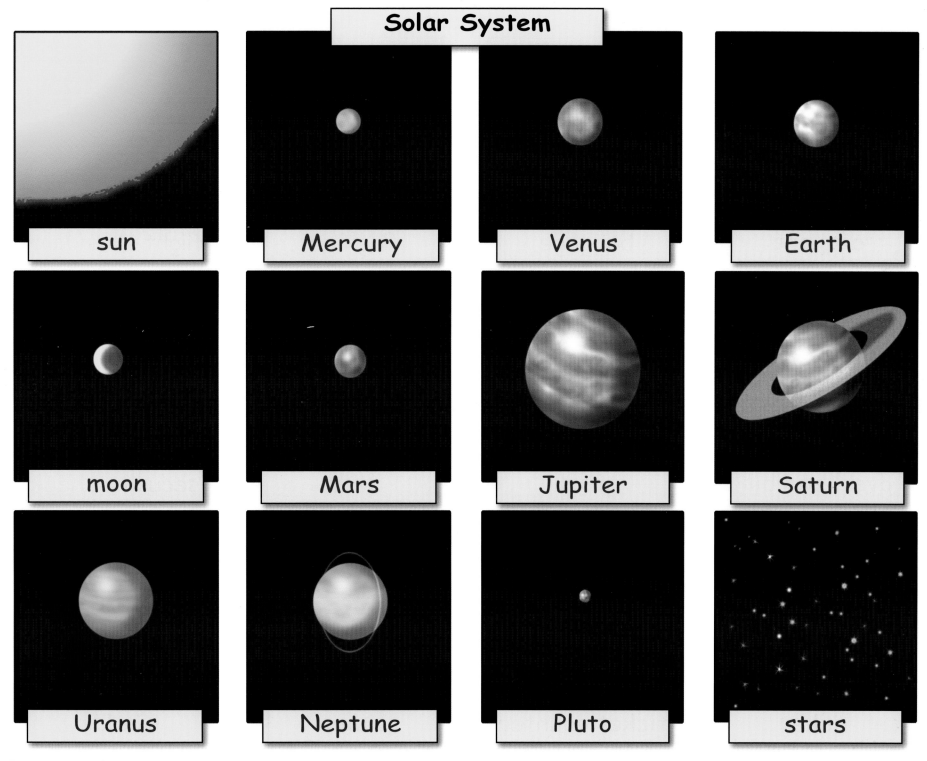

Solar System

sun

Mercury

Venus

Earth

moon

Mars

Jupiter

Saturn

Uranus

Neptune

Pluto

stars

Airport

airplane

baggage

flagman

flight attendant

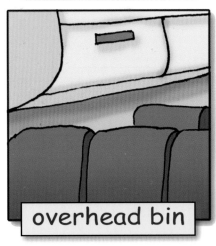

overhead bin

pilot

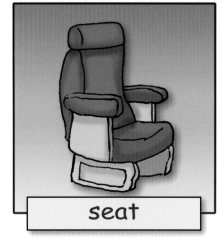

seat

security check

ticket

ticket counter

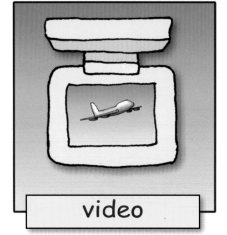

video

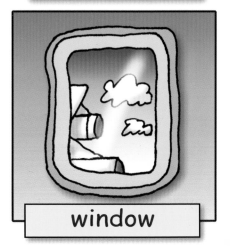

window

The Theater

actor

backstage

costumes

curtain

director

dressing room

lights

make-up

orchestra pit

program

script

stage

Garden

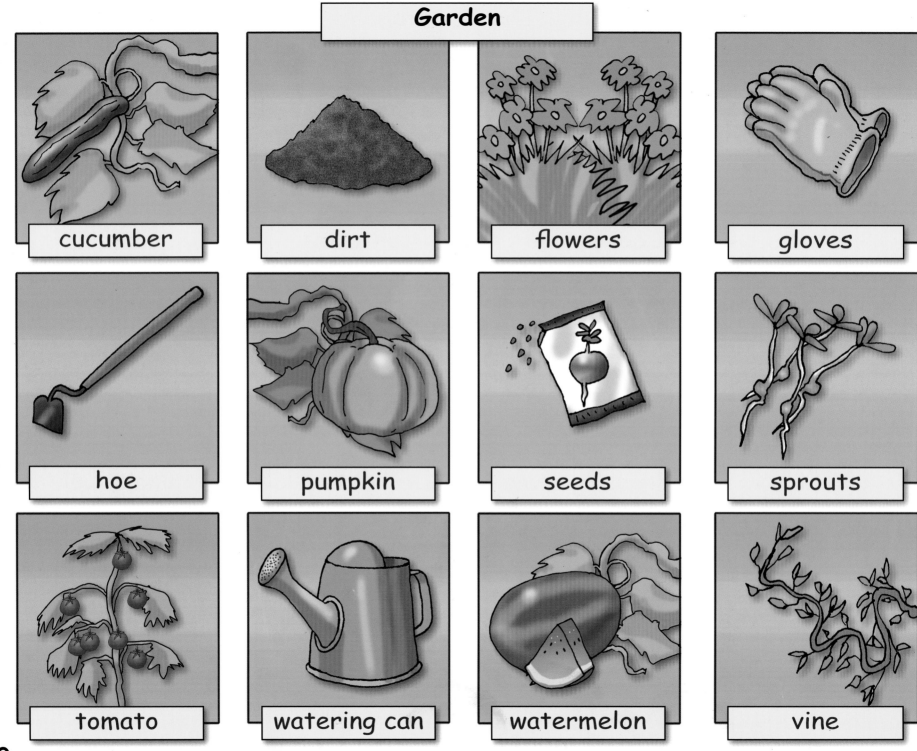

cucumber

dirt

flowers

gloves

hoe

pumpkin

seeds

sprouts

tomato

watering can

watermelon

vine

100

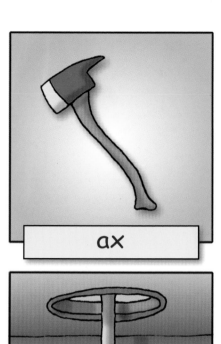

ax

boots

dog

fire

firepole

fire truck

hat

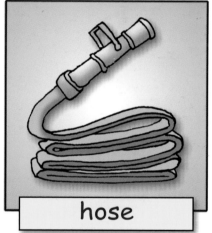

hose

jacket

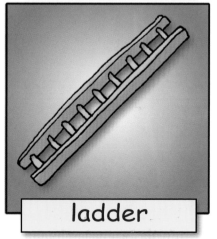

ladder

smoke

station

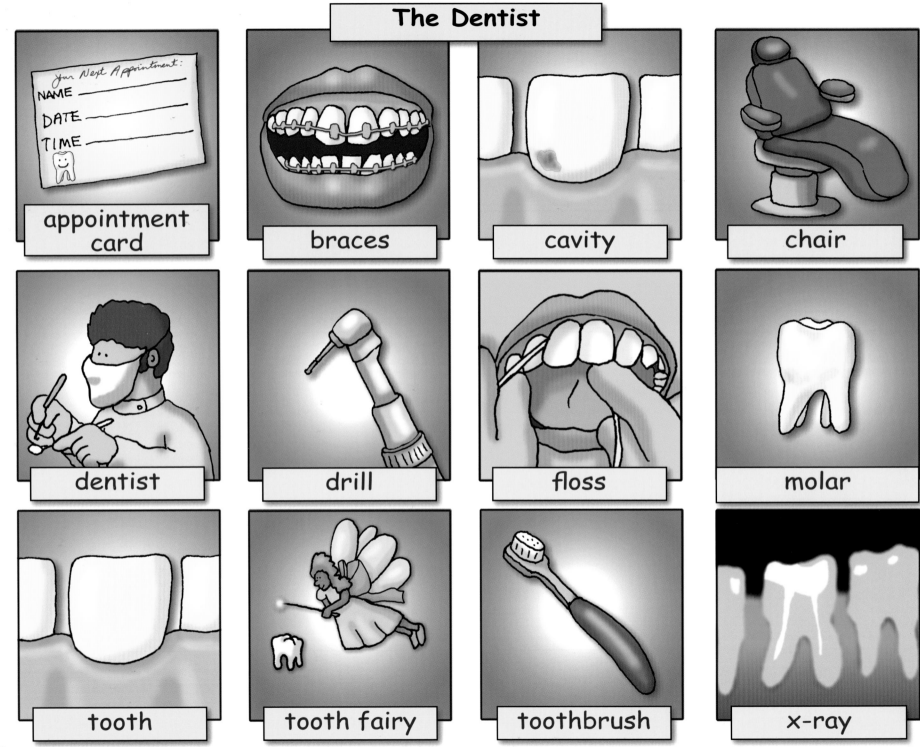

The Dentist

appointment card

braces

cavity

chair

dentist

drill

floss

molar

tooth

tooth fairy

toothbrush

x-ray

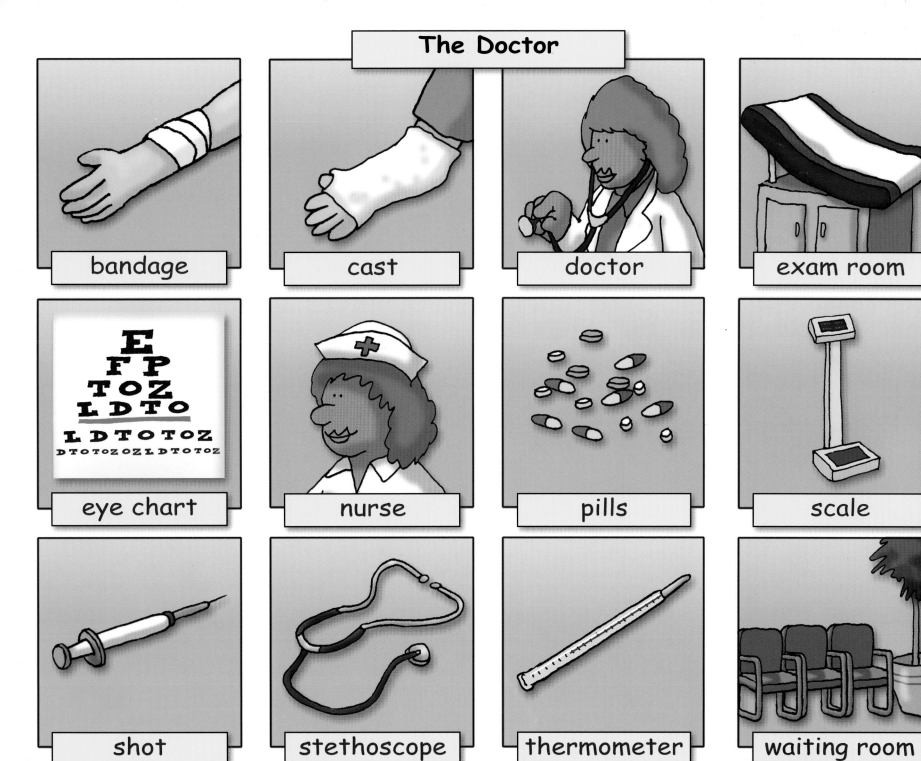

The Doctor

bandage

cast

doctor

exam room

eye chart

nurse

pills

scale

shot

stethoscope

thermometer

waiting room

Construction

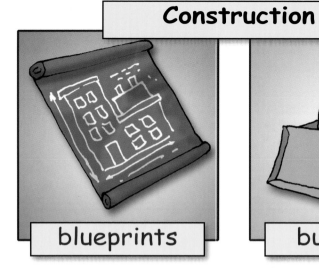
backhoe

blueprints

bulldozer

cement truck

crane

dump truck

forklift

hard hat

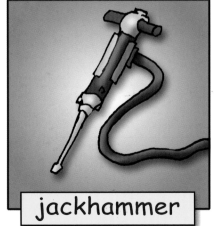
jackhammer

lunchbox

welder

worker

Birds

bluebird

cardinal

crow

duck

eagle

goose

hawk

hummingbird

owl

seagull

sparrow

woodpecker

The Forest

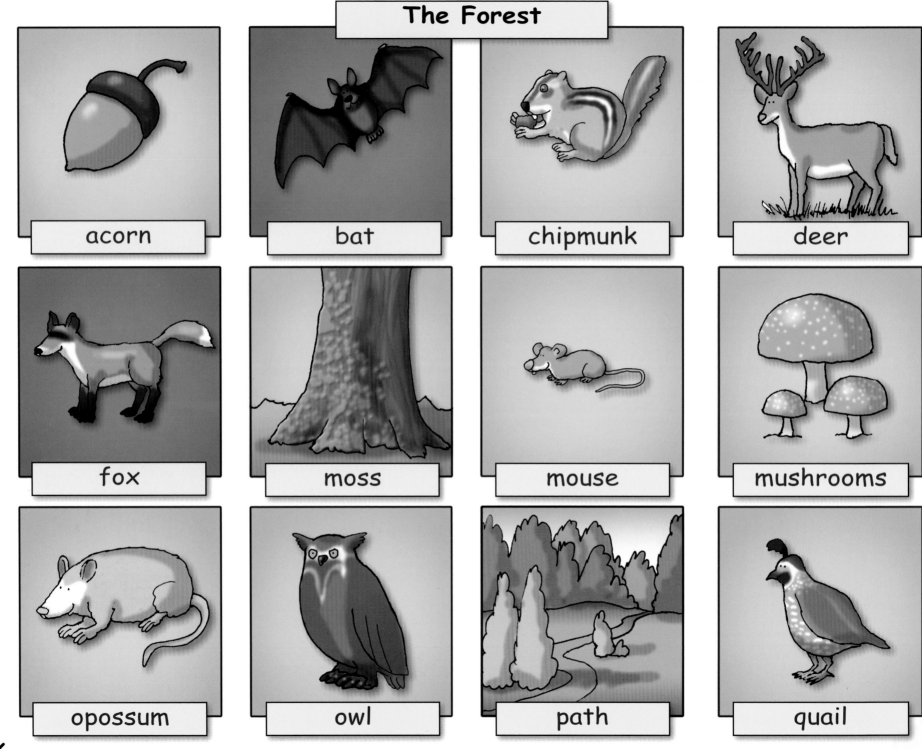

acorn

bat

chipmunk

deer

fox

moss

mouse

mushrooms

opossum

owl

path

quail

The Forest

rabbit

raccoon

seeds

skunk

snake

squirrel

toad

trees

turkey

vulture

weasel

wolf

The City

bench

bridge

bus

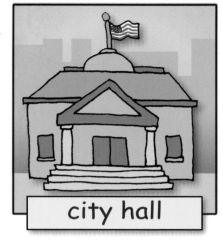
city hall

elevated train

hot dog stand

park

policeman

skyscraper

subway

taxi

traffic

Daredevils

broncobuster

deep sea diver

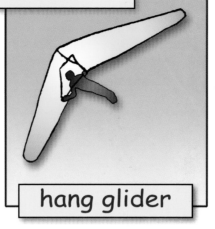
hang glider

lion tamer

monster truck driver

motorcycle jumper

mountain climber

race car driver

rock wall climber

skate ramp jumper

skydiver

surfer

109

Vacation

camera

car

credit card

DVD player

gas station

map

pillow

post card

road

road sign

souvenir

tourist

110

Index